Spirituality in the Gospel of Thomas

FRONT COVER:
Detail from sixth century icon[2] of
Jesus at the monastery church of
Saint Catherine, Mount Sinai.

BY THE SAME AUTHOR:

The Gospel of Thomas
Newly presented to bring out the
meaning, with Introductions,
Paraphrases and Notes

Introducing the Gospel of Thomas

Thirty Essays on the Gospel of Thomas

Jesus untouched by the Church
His Teachings in the Gospel of Thomas

George Fox speaks for Himself

George Fox a Christian Mystic

Pegasus the Seminal Early Computer

Also the websites at
www.gospelofthomas.info
www.gospelofthomas.net

Spirituality in the Gospel of Thomas

By Hugh McGregor Ross

Calligraphy by John Blamires

A Bright Pen Book
Published 2010

Text, format and presentation copyright © Hugh McGregor Ross 1998 and 2010.

The Gospel itself in Part II done in hand-drawn calligraphy by John Blamires, and first published in 1998 by Sessions of York, York, England.

All rights reserved. No part of this publication may be reproduced, stored in a retrieval system, or transmitted, in any form or by any means, electronic, mechanical, photocopying, recording or otherwise, without the prior permission of the copyright owner. Nor can it be circulated in any form of binding or cover other than that in which it is published and without similar condition including this condition being imposed on a subsequent purchaser.

Catalogue records for this book are available from the British Library and the Library of Congress.

Text typeset by the author in Baskerville and *MediciSkript*

ISBN 978 07552 1268 2

Authors Online Ltd
19 The Cinques,
Gamlinglay, Sandy,
Bedfordshire SG19 1NU, England

Printed and bound by Lightning Source.

*Written for Martin and Clare
and completed in memory of Clare.*

Contents

PART I
Starting you on the Discovery

Introduction	page 3
Starting Out	5
Practical Matters	10
Spirituality, the Ultimate Attribute	13
A Direct Way Forward	16

PART II
The Teachings

The Good News Brought by Thomas	21
The Summary	22
Discrimination	26
Seeing the Master	31
Turning to the Master	40
To Know and Metanoïa	42
Birth and Death	49
Light at the Centre	52
Finding the Light at the Centre	54
Quenching Ahamkāra	56
Oneness	73
Spiritual Life Essential	85
From Small Things Great Grow	87
The Way to the Kingdom	89
Spiritual Richness	97
Monakhos and Courage	101
Happiness	105

Images	111
Old Order and New Way	117
Beyond Femininity	124
Wealth in Poverty	127
Simplicity of Living	128
Jesus' Disappointment	130
Wise Sayings	135
The Consummation	138

Part III
Reflections

Preface to these Reflections	145
Searching and Finding	146
Treasure Hunt	148
A Direct Path based on Experience	151
Quenching its Power	159
The Indian Similarity	162
Dwell in the Light	168
Empty Desert ?	169
Opening the Door	171
The Jewel	173
A Sparkling Analogy	175
The Inherent Light Within	178
Beyond Any Words	180
Removing the Mountain	182
The Big Question—Or Is It ?	184
A Creative Mantra	186
Bibliography and Notes	188
Index to the Logia	194
Annex – The 'Thomas' Collection	199

Part I

Starting you on the Discovery

Introduction

Spirituality is all those experiences that lie beyond the body, beyond the mind, beyond the senses, and which enrich your life.

This book helps you discover the spiritual treasures that are hidden in the Gospel of Thomas. With its help you can discover by yourself spiritual truths that Jesus offered to mankind.

The Gospel of Thomas concentrates on the rôle of Jesus as a spiritual Teacher. We can discern that the ancient manuscript discovered in Egypt was not a literary composition, but is a collection of the sayings of Jesus[3]. This implies that the apostle Thomas recalled them from his memory and recorded them by dictating them to a scribe, a common practice in those times.

Jesus shared his spiritual awareness through the medium of parables. It may be called his teaching technique. You will already be familiar with some of his major parables—the good samaritan, the lost sheep, the prodigal son. However, in the Gospel of Thomas every saying that Thomas recorded is a mini-parable. Each one has an outer form, referring to everyday things, some of which related specifically to the time and place of Jesus and the people he moved amongst. Yet within each one is an element or component of his spiritual teaching—these have a timeless quality, and hence are applicable to us today.

Thus the process of deriving benefit from the Gospel of Thomas consists firstly on bringing forth these hidden inner

INTRODUCTION

meanings of Jesus' sayings. The Gospel is quite specific about this, placing emphasis on seeking and an even greater emphasis on finding. One of the fascinating things about this is that it's most meaningful when you find the inner meaning of a saying for yourself. It's noteworthy that in this Gospel neither Jesus nor Thomas give any explanations of the mini-parables. In practice, the greatest impact occurs when you can exclaim "So that's what he means".

This book gives you countless clues and hints to help you find these inner meanings.

However, it goes further than that in a different way. One of the consequences of the sayings being merely recalled from memory to be dictated to a scribe is that there is no discernible order or pattern in the ancient Gospel. A feature of this book is that the sayings have been rearranged to put those with like-for-like meanings together. In doing this the sayings have not been tampered with or modified in any way, and every one in the ancient document has been included.

So what you will find are groups of sayings which, together, reveal a spiritual teaching given by Jesus. His teachings are brought out from their hiding. As you read and preferably speak aloud the words of Jesus your inborn inner spiritual ear will be enlivened. Then as you become accustomed to his idiom your third or spiritual eye will be opened, and you will gradually be drawn into the presence of one of the Great Souls who have come to share their spiritual awareness with you and all mankind.

Starting Out

The best way to start out with the Gospel of Thomas is to *assume* that the opening lines mean what they say. Here they are:

> *These are the hidden logia which the living Jesus spoke and Judas Didymos Thomas recorded.*

They mean that as the apostle Thomas walked around with Jesus he heard these sayings and recorded them.

It is not a matter of believing them to be true. No-where in this Gospel does Jesus ask you to believe in anything, he even derides belief and replaces it by knowing. Yet we have no means of knowing that the opening lines are true. Nor is it a matter of asking the opinion of anyone else, whether that person might be regarded as an expert, or something you have read on the internet. It is purely a matter of making an assumption, of carrying out a kind of experiment, and of waiting to see whether these sayings, as their meanings gradually reveal themselves to you, come to have a living quality as the words of a Great Soul. If they speak to you, that is sufficient.

If these sayings and teachings come alive in you, well and good. If they don't the experiment will not work for you, just let it be, just lay 'Thomas' down and go back to where you were before. You may later feel the urge to pick up 'Thomas' again—do so! This time it may come alive for you.

STARTING OUT

With that as a starting point, consider the first sayings which—unusually for this Gospel—form a group. You will find later that these give a kind of summary, encapsulate the quintessence, of the Gospel and its teachings. But for the time being study them carefully in the light of the notes and explanations that have been added. What you will be learning to do is to recognize important and distinctive features of the way Jesus spoke, of the idioms he used and how his thinking went. In short, you will be learning how in his speech Jesus passed on his awareness of the spiritual to his hearers. Notice how he spoke in short phrases. How sometimes these are given in a hierarchical sequence of increasing significance. Notice also how sometimes a saying will make one statement and then follow it with the opposite. This is always done so that the second heightens the impact or the import of the first.

You will see Jesus' extensive use of symbolic language. This is primarily because he is trying to convey concepts that cannot be pinned down in mere words, so that all that the words can do is to act as pointers to something beyond, that he is urging you to grasp.

Everyone has initially found these sayings difficult; there is no exception to this rule. It comes about primarily because Jesus speaks in 'Thomas' from a high spiritual level and we are only groping around below him.

Unlike the first group of sayings, which are a kind of outline or summary of the whole of 'Thomas', and for which the fullest meaning will only become apparent when you are very familiar with all the teachings, the next group in this book are brought together from many places in the original Gospel. In one way or another they show that Jesus was teaching his hearers about discrimination or discernment. This is not really a spiritual topic in itself, for it is much more something done with the mind, a taking of the most beneficial decisions when a choice has to be made. However, in some other spiritual traditions than our Western culture it is regarded as an essential entry-point, a basic practice, for finding the spiritual way forward. You will find, furthermore, once the ability to exercise this kind of discrimination has been acquired, with an appropriate guiding light, that it will prove to be very valuable in many ordinary situations of life.

When you turn to this group of sayings you will encounter one of the crucial features of using 'Thomas'. It is the simple one that when you come across a saying that, having given it some little time of thought, does not speak to you in some way, just by-pass it. This may well be because it does not 'speak to your condition' at that moment. It is far better to put it on one side and let it wait until you can come back to it later. You will also soon find another feature that for you some sayings have more impact, more meaning, more significance than others. This variability is of course an inevitable aspect of any collection, whether sayings or works of art or pieces of music.

You can learn a lot more of the idiom Jesus used, how he constructed his sayings, and his way of thinking from the first of the sayings given in this second group, the story of the fisherman. It starts with the words The Man, where in this book man is spelled with a capital letter. That is to alert you to the word having a special meaning, in this case a man who has learnt the art and practice of discrimination. Then note that he is likened to a wise fisherman. Jesus even repeats this later, whereas usually you have to pay great attention to every single word he says. It is to emphasize the idea of discrimination.

STARTING OUT

This wise fisherman chose the large fine fish without difficulty or trouble or hesitation or doubt or query within himself. The 'wise' at the start of the saying and the 'without difficulty' at the finish make the saying into a whole. But more than that, the juxtaposition of those two ideas contains and conveys the very essence of the saying, what Jesus is telling you, the aspect of his Teaching that he is trying to share with you.

Symbolically, of course, the large fine fish refers to Jesus, and the great number of small fish represent all the other spiritual teachers. In our day there may be even more of these than in his, with a great variety of their man-made, own-brand teachings. But note that this wise fisherman did not just throw them back into the sea to drift away with the tide. He threw them to the bottom of the sea. The man—or the woman nowadays—being wise, ultimately and absolutely rejected those lesser teachers.

There is another feature of Jesus' thought and speaking that you will come to later, for example in logion #64 the story of the man inviting guests to a dinner, or in logion #47 where he emphasizes that the new replaces the old, or in the special logion #22 about finding Oneness. Here Jesus takes an idea and expresses it again and again in different words. Usually the sequence builds up to some kind of climax, just as in the sayings with a hierarchical sequence of phrases. But the main feature is his reiteration of the basic idea, to really drive it home.

Be watchful for the sayings, there are many of them, in which the words at the start relate to those at the finish. As you link these together you will find the key that will give you the real meaning of the saying.

All these explanations have been given so you may become aware of, may tune into, the idioms that Jesus uses. However it is specially noticeable that no-where in 'Thomas' is there any explanation of any of the parables. The reason for this is that the meaning of each saying has most impact, it is most beneficial in your coming to an awareness of the spirituality Jesus was aiming to give you, when you find the inner meanings for yourself.

Jesus in his parables presents you with what can be likened to puzzles. The only thing you need is to have the urge to seek out the intended meanings on your own. Explanations and commentaries on the sayings by other people dull the edge of this exploration, even take away the experience of inner transformation that they offer. Please do not be put off by this. Many people have worked their way through the initial apparent difficulties in these sayings and then on finding the inner meanings have reached the experience that the teachings are surprisingly simple. This is because, once awakened to them, they chime with something deep inside you, they ring true. You will just know they are right and valuable.

There is one further guideline that will help you. It is to check that the meaning you come up with for any single saying is harmonious with the meanings of all the others. This is because all these sayings are given by one Great Soul, and he must have been harmonious and consistent within himself. Also, in this book the grouping of the sayings into teachings, and the multitude of clues that are given, will guide you on your way.

Practical Matters

In using this book you will find it beneficial to keep in mind the following points.

The ancient document we have of the Gospel of Thomas that was dug up in Egypt is written as a unbroken string of letters. It was done before spaces between words had been invented. There are no punctuation marks, which have had to be added. There are just a few signs to aid pronunciation. This is an indication that it was primarily meant to be read aloud—it was done before many people could read. You, too, will find it helpful to read each saying aloud to yourself.[4]

The sayings were identified and numbered by the first Western scholars to study the Gospel, Professor Guilles Quispel and his colleagues. Within each saying the French Métanoïa scholars identified and numbered the short phrases. They are copied in this book. These short phrases are a characteristic of Jesus' way of speaking, and were often helpful, sometimes essential, in discerning the intended meaning. (In the Bible they survive only in the Lord's Prayer.)

Jesus often used ordinary words with an enhanced meaning. In this book they have been given an initial capital letter. When you come across one of those, to get the right meaning it needs to be pronounced with emphasis, or when reading halt and ask yourself "Why has that word been given a capital letter?"

PRACTICAL MATTERS

You will have noticed that as a form of shorthand the Gospel of Thomas is written as 'Thomas'. But when reference is being made to the apostle Thomas himself the quotation marks are omitted.

You will also have noticed small numbers in the text. They are references to items in the Bibliography and Notes at the far end of the book. These are of informative value, not spiritual.

In 'Thomas' Jesus had much to say about women, and you will find it very pleasing. However, when he wished to refer equally to a man or a woman he used the masculine convention. This has been copied in this book. Therefore if you are a woman, whenever you see he/him/his read it as she/her/hers.

A more subtle feature is in the use of the word 'shall'. It is more than indicating the future tense. So when you read it invest it with the old English meaning of a command or a promise.

In the ancient document there is no discernible pattern in the sequence of the sayings recorded by Thomas. However in this book they have been grouped together with like-for-like meanings. After most groups (but not all) some notes have been added where experience shows they may be helpful for your understanding. It has been found that for some topics or teaching no notes are needed.

One of the distinctive features of 'Thomas' is that it uses words very precisely. That is to say, each and every word carries exactly its own meaning, there is no fuzziness nor ambiguity. This is only to be expected from the words of a Master.[5] On the other hand, there are numerous occasions when Jesus has used synonyms, usually in each case with a slightly different nuance or associated meaning. In 'Thomas' Jesus uses many synonyms to refer to the nature of spiritual truth: the All, One, Unity, the Kingdom, Life,

Light, the Living, the Father, Kingdom of the Father, the Father and the Mother, the Pure Spirit, Kingdom of the heavens.

Part of this precise use of words, combined with the use of synonyms, derives from the fact that Jesus was sometimes speaking to Jewish people and at other times to the Hellenist people who comprised nine out of ten of the population of his time and place.[6] These people lived in a society and environment largely influenced by Greek practices, were familiar with Greek concepts and ways of thinking and, in particular, knew the meaning of distinctive Greek words. We must assume that Jesus was bilingual in his mother tongue of Aramaic and also in Greek. It is apparent that Jesus adapted his speech, and especially the use of important or key-words, to suit his listeners on each occasion.

For some of these concepts, and in certain other instances, no word in the English language exists. Therefore here foreign words are employed. It is found to be very much better gradually to come to understand their meanings, than to use English renderings that can only be inadequate or misleading.

Spirituality, the Ultimate Attribute

Man, meaning mankind in general, may be said to be distinguished from all other living creatures by having three attributes or qualities. Traces of them may perhaps exist in some of the other creatures, but in man they dominate.

It is often said that in the evolutionary process man became first distinguishable as a tool-maker. Of course then only very rudimentary tools, perhaps a stone tied to a stick, but we can easily see the progression[7] to our modern achievements of atomic generation of electricity or of computers.

The second distinction lies in man's intellectual ability. This has led to the great philosophies and the sciences, the capacity to contemplate the majestic nature of the universe, and what seems to be the distinctive awareness of time—some suggest this being engendered by the foresight needed to plant seeds as preliminaries to the harvest.

The third distinctive attribute is the spiritual. All the evidence indicates that this is unique to mankind. In particular, this gives the capability for mankind to become aware of spirits, gods or the one God, as some would say; or as others would say, to conceive of them[8]—a product or projection of our innate quality.

In each of these respects individuals differ in their capability, just as when we consider sub-divisions of these attributes we see greater or lesser craftsmen and craftswomen, philosophers or psychologists, artists and musicians, doctors and dancers. So it is also in the spiritual.

SPIRITUALITY, THE ULTIMATE ATTRIBUTE

During the centuries there have arisen persons in whom the spiritual attribute has excelled. These are the Great Souls of mankind, it being generally recognized that amongst them are Krishna, Buddha, perhaps Confucius, Moses, Mohammed, Guru Singh and Jesus. They not only manifested to a high degree the spiritual attribute of mankind, but were also prepared to share that awareness with others.

When we turn to the Gospel of Thomas we find in it one of the means by which Jesus shared his awareness of the spiritual, with his teachings expressed primarily in the form of parables.

Such sharing could only be effective when there is some quality common both to the giver and the recipient—it is your innate indwelling distinctive attribute of spirituality. This is the medium for the communication. That the attribute is great in the giver and only small in the recipient does not alter the fact of there being a common attribute.

In the phraseology used in this book that attribute is termed the Real Self. So as these sayings of Jesus awaken you to the Real Self within, you are becoming aware of what might be called the collective Real Self of all mankind. You may have qualms—and they are legitimate ones—about the greatness and the smallness of that attribute, but that is only the superimposition of the concept of quantity upon what is qualitatively one and the same.

Spirituality or spiritual Truth is not something that can be known or grasped or appreciated with the mind, for it is an experience that is beyond the mind and the intellect. It is the greatest experience of which the human being is capable—it may even be called Experience itself.

SPIRITUALITY, THE ULTIMATE ATTRIBUTE

It is communicated to any person seeking it by being in the presence of another who has attained it to a greater degree. Thomas found that experience by being in the presence of one of the Great Souls of mankind in whom spiritual Life and vitality glowed and shone to its ultimate degree. He shared or attained that awareness to such an extent that he earned the nickname or epithet of the Twin.[9]

We know Thomas went on to share it with others who in turn shared it in a kind of chain-reaction until a great community evolved, spread over several countries.[10] At some stage he must have realized that there would be value in recording some of the sayings he remembered being spoken by Jesus. This created what we now have as the Gospel of Thomas. They were stepping stones in the path of his spiritual development or attainment that he regarded as important. Your spiritual path may also benefit by following in his footsteps.

While great respect is due to man's achievements with his material and intellectual attributes, as a person interested in the spiritual you may well feel this third one to be paramount. There have certainly been individuals who have had the experience that when the spiritual side of life is strong, then all other aspects are healthy. In particular, the great spiritual qualities of happiness or joyousness, and of tranquility or inner peace.

Thus it may well be best to shift your stance, your perspective, your attention to your spiritual attribute, which is your birthright, your Place, your very inner nature, and from there seek to come into the company and presence of a Great Soul who has already manifested that quality.

Thus you can come into the real world of the spiritual. It is Reality itself, and you are an inhabitant of it.

A Direct Way Forward

The Gospel of Thomas offers you a direct link between one of the Great Souls of mankind and the most essential attribute in you, the very essence of humanity in you.

This link is direct. It is unmediated, not influenced by or tampered with by anyone. It has a purity, it is immediate.

It comes from, and goes to, that spiritual place within you that lies beyond or by-passes the influence and interference of the mind. There is no need to get involved with complex philosophies or speculations. The mind and the intellect can rest in peace.

It is something that is offered, it is not imposed. To attain it you only need to seek it. Assurance is given that it shall be found. This is because it is calling upon, and responding to, a quality that is inherently within you.

Part of the work of a great Teacher such as Jesus is to awaken the quality, the capability within you, to respond to what is being offered. This is not that you are being taught something new, for it is a capability that has always been there, merely lying dormant. It is inherently latent within you.

When it is aroused and satisfied a whole cornucopia of blessings follow. Your life becomes enriched by happiness, by recognition of beauty, by certainty and absence of doubt. Perhaps most of all a way is provided to surmount and overcome the pains and distress of suffering, whether this arises from disorders of the body or of the mind.

DIRECT WAY FORWARD

* * *

You will find there are several sayings in which the "disciples"—who probably were those we call the apostles who walked about with Jesus—ask questions. In each case these arose from the baggage of old ideas they carried about with them. In 'Thomas' however Jesus never answers negatively, never chides nor rebukes. His answers are always positive, to lead them on to some better awareness, to replace the old idea with something new. It is inevitable that you also will have doubts or uncertainties arising from the luggage you bring. Rather than these being blown away, leaving a painful vacuum, you will find some positive new awareness such that old concepts merely fade away.[11]

Part II

The Teachings

A disciple expresses his affection and gratitude to his revered Teacher.

ΠΕΥΑΓΓΕΛΙΟΝ ΠΚΑΤΑΘΩΜΑC

The Good News Brought by Thomas

Try to imagine you are meeting Jesus, being unaware of, and uncontaminated by, ideas about him from the Church or elsewhere, being only aware that you are coming into the presence of a Great Soul.

This is what you might hear.

At the top is a facsimile of the colophon added by the scribe at the end of the ancient document. Unlike our practice of writing the title at the start of a book, they put it after the finish.

It is a mixture of Greek and Coptic, and its literal translation is added below it.

The monk may have put it there as an exclamation of praise!

The Summary

1. These are the hidden logia
2. which the living Jesus spoke
3. and Didymos Judas Thomas recorded.

1

1. And he said:
2. He who finds the inner meaning of these logia
3. will find life independent of death.

2

Jesus said:
1. Let him who seeks not cease from seeking
2. until he finds;
3. and when he finds,
4. he will be disturbed,
5. and when he is disturbed
6. he will marvel
7. and he shall reign over the All.

3

1. Jesus said:
2. If those who guide your Being say to you:
3. "Behold the Kingdom is in the heaven,"
4. then the birds of the sky will precede you;
5. if they say to you: "It is in the sea,"
6. then the fish will precede you.
7. But the Kingdom is in your centre
8. and is about you.
9. When you Know your Selves
10. then you will be Known,
11. and you will be aware that you are
12. the sons of the Living Father.
13. But if you do not Know yourselves
14. then you are in poverty,
15. and you are the poverty.

THE SUMMARY

The opening statement of the ancient document seems to be by Thomas himself. In the first place, it tells us he was another Judas, this would be his birth-name. However he had also been given, whether by Jesus or his fellow-disciples we cannot tell, the Greek name Didymos and the Aramaic name Thomas. These both mean 'twin'. It was, and still is, a common practice to give spiritual names like this, and we have to regard them as being a recognition of his spiritual affinity or twin-ship to Jesus.

'Logia', the plural of logion (pronounced with a soft-g) is a saying imbued with a spiritual meaning. Thomas refers to them as being "hidden"[12] with the symbolic meaning that there is a deeper meaning within each one than first meets the eye. We now call these parables.

The "living Jesus" means exactly what it says.[12] Thomas heard these sayings as he went about with Jesus during his travelling ministry and later recorded them by dictation to a scribe.[13]

We cannot tell whether the next saying is a comment by Thomas, born of his experience, or is an assertion by Jesus. The significance is the same, you are about to come upon sayings that reveal a special kind of Life that has nothing to do with mortal life.

The saying numbered 2 starts us on those by Jesus. In the first place, notice his characteristic use of short phrases. This saying also reveals another of his practices, for the phrases are arranged in a hierarchical sequence, of increasing import—seeking, finding, being disturbed (which may well be disconcerting), marvelling, (which is truly rewarding) and reigning.

So long as you have the urge to seek, you will come back again and again to this very simple yet very profound saying.

THE SUMMARY

The next, longer, saying tells quite a lot more about Jesus and his way of teaching. To begin with, in phrases 2 to 6, he is having some fun lampooning the false teachers who abounded then, and still do. Then suddenly he arrests us by the profound statement of phrases 7 and 8. Here of course he is speaking symbolically, by using the word Kingdom. He is alluding, for his Jewish listeners, to the greatest, most glorious, most majestic condition they could conceive of.

He consolidates that in phrases 9 to 12, and then we find another very characteristic feature of his way of speaking. He suddenly presents the opposite, but done in such a way as to highlight and emphasize the previous thoughts.

To get the full impact you have to be careful to read the last phrase correctly: it is not just poverty, but the spiritual poverty itself.

Thomas must have had some purpose, some intent, in marshaling and putting together this group of sayings at the start of his Gospel, for in a crucial way they sum up what lies at the heart of it. He may well have put this group together in his mind before he started his dictation; other sayings follow just as he recalled them individually. To extract the full meaning and significance of this initial group it is necessary to become familiar with teachings that are expounded later. So in this book this Summary is repeated at the finish[14] of Part II.

After this initial group of sayings Thomas must have let his memory range more widely, for subsequent sayings in the ancient document are not in any discernible order or pattern.[15]

Discrimination

8
1. And he said:
2. The Man is like a wise fisherman
3. who cast his net into the sea;
4. he drew it up from the sea full of small fish.
5. Amongst them,
6. he found one large and fine fish.
7. That wise fisherman, he cast all the small fish
      down to the bottom of the sea,
8. he chose the large fish without difficulty.
9. He who has ears to hear let him hear!

107
1. Jesus said:
2. The Kingdom is like a shepherd
3. who owned a hundred sheep.
4. One among them, which was the largest,
                    went astray;

DISCRIMINATION

(107)
5 he left the ninety-nine,
6 he sought after the one
7 until he found it.
8 When he had toiled,
9 he said to that sheep:
10 I desire you more than the ninety-nine!

76
1 Jesus said:
2 The Kingdom of the Father is like a man, a merchant,
3 who owned merchandise,
4 and found a pearl.
5 That merchant was wise:
6 he sold the merchandise,
7 he bought this one single pearl for himself.
8 You also, seek after the treasure
9 which does not perish,
10 which remains in the place
11 where no moth comes near to devour,
12 and no worm destroys.

DISCRIMINATION

36

1. Jesus said:
2. Have no care, from morning until evening
3. and from evening until morning,
4. for what you will put on.

14

1. Jesus said to them:
2. If you fast you will do
3. something prejudicial to yourselves,
4. and if you pray
5. you will be condemned,
6. and if you give alms
7. you will do harm to your spirits.
8. And as you go into every land
9. and wander in the countryside,
10. if they receive you,
11. eat what they set before you,
12. heal the sick amongst them.
13. For what goes into your mouth
14. will not defile you,
15. but what comes out of your mouth,
16. that is what will defile you.

89

1 Jesus said:
2 Why do you wash the outside of the cup?
3 Do you not understand
4 that He who made the inside
5 is also He who made the outside.

Jesus gives us a number of sayings about the need and use in the spiritual life of the quality of discrimination—using that word with the meaning of discrimination between, not discriminating against. It is very near to the meaning of discernment.

In the West it is little emphasized. No teacher at school, no lecturer at college, no preacher in the pulpit, encourages his

DISCRIMINATION

hearers to become adept at discrimination, lest it leads to thinking "What nonsense he speaks!" But, specially in the Eastern spiritual tradition, it is the first thing to be taught.

It consists of developing the practice of being able to distinguish between what is spiritually valuable and what is not; in making the choice between two ideas, two teachings, two courses of action, which may look much the same, but only one will be the more rewarding or beneficial. It may be likened to walking in the country and coming to a fork or crossing in the paths, and being able to choose the right one. It is akin to developing good judgement. More specifically, and at the deep spiritual level, it means having the ability to distinguish the Real from the non-Real. In 'Thomas' Jesus encourages you to develop that skill.

This type of discrimination is of course important in many aspects of life. It is just that in the spiritual it's harder to acquire.

There are two corollaries to this. The first relates to superimposition. This is taught in the Indian tradition by the analogy of walking along a narrow country path in the dusk, always somewhat dicey. Suddenly you spy a snake coiled in your path! But on closer cautious inspection it is revealed as a coil of rope. You had superimposed the snake on the rope.

The second is more subtle. Discrimination is an art or skill or practice that is essentially done by yourself. Yet to be effective and rewarding it needs to be done in the guidance or light of a spiritual Teacher. The Teacher is not telling you what choice to make, but is giving you the background or capability for you to make the right choice.

In the Gospel of Thomas, Jesus offers himself in that rôle.

Seeing the Master

5
1. Jesus said:
2. Know Him who is before your face,
3. and what is hidden from you shall be revealed to you:
4. for there is nothing hidden that shall not be manifest.

17
1. Jesus said:
2. I will give you what no eye has seen,
3. and what no ear has heard,
4. and what no hand has touched,
5. and what has not arisen in the heart of man.

15

1. Jesus said:
2. When you behold
3. Him who was not begotten of woman,
4. prostrate yourselves upon your face
5. and worship him;
6. that one is your Father.

59

1. Jesus said:
2. Look upon Him who is living
3. as long as you live,
4. lest you should die
5. and you should seek to see Him;
6. and you would not be able to see.

79

1. A woman from the multitude said to him:
2. Fortunate is the womb that bore you
3. and the breasts that nourished you.
4. He said to her:
5. Fortunate are they who have heard the Logos of the Father,
6. and have kept it in truth.
7. For there will be days when you will say:
8. Fortunate is the womb that did not conceive
9. and the breasts that did not suckle.

82

1. Jesus said:
2. He who is near to me is near to the fire,
3. and he who is far from me is far from the Kingdom.

77

1. Jesus said:
2. I am the Light that is above all things.
3. I am the All.
4. The All comes forth from me,
5. and the All extends throughout me.
6. Cleave the wood, I am there;
7. raise the stone,
8. and you shall find me there.

108

1. Jesus said:
2. He who drinks from my mouth
3. shall become as me;
4. and I myself will become him,
5. and the hidden things shall be manifested.

13

1. Jesus said to his disciples:
2. Make a comparison to me
3. and tell me whom I resemble.
4. Simon Peter said to him:
5. You resemble a righteous angel.
6. Matthew said to him:
7. You resemble a wise man, a philosopher.
8. Thomas said to him:
9. Master, my mouth will absolutely not permit
10. me to say you resemble anyone.
11. Jesus said:
12. I am not your Master;
13. because you have drunk,
14. you have become enlivened from the bubbling spring
15. which I have made to gush out.
16. He took him aside,
17. and spoke three logia to him.
18. Now, when Thomas had returned to his companions,
19. they questioned him:
20. What did Jesus say to you?
21. Thomas said to them:

(13)
²² If I tell you one of the logia that he said to me,
²³ you will take up stones
²⁴ and throw them against me;
²⁵ and fire will come forth from the stones
²⁶ and burn you up.

Jesus invites you into his presence! "Know Him who is before your face . . . . . Look upon Him who is living". Not of course to know a mortal man, tied to one point in time and space. Nor to look in some imaginary way on a resurrected spirit—there is no hint of that in 'Thomas'. But to come into the presence of a Great Soul manifesting the spiritual attribute of mankind, and see with your third or spiritual eye. This is your own innate possession of that spiritual quality, however feeble and dimmed it may be. Giver and receiver being on the same wavelength, communication is established in that presence, and enrichment takes place. Thus he speaks of that spiritual attribute "The All comes forth from me, and the All reaches towards me".

As he speaks in various ways of this communication between Master and seeker within that presence, he offers those who imbibe and assimilate his words a supreme union

He who drinks from my mouth
shall become as me;
and I myself will become him.

This gives the ultimate mystical experience. Perhaps it may only be found during profound contemplation; the clue is to recognize that the feeling of his majesty and your minuscule being is a mere superimposition due to a lack of discrimination.

It will greatly assist you to see with your inner eye and to come into the presence of a Great Soul if you obtain a copy, the best you can get, of an icon of Jesus from the Eastern Orthodox church.[16]

Let this be kept in a special place in your home. Maintain living flowers beside it. Each day spend some time before it, gazing intently in contemplation or focussed meditation. Then it will gradually come alive for you, and you will be drawn into his presence.

This, more than anything else, is all the practice that is needed.

The saying that starts:

Make a comparison to me (logion 13)

is the only autobiographical one in 'Thomas'. As a true disciple Thomas would know he must record faithfully, and must not intrude elsewhere. Thomas tells of an episode which, when combined with related passages from the gospels in the Bible (Matthew 16:13, Mark 8:27, Luke 9:18), other contemporary documents, and what can be seen today, can be very easily visualized.

After his initial ministry around the Lake of Galilee and having gathered some disciples, Jesus might have suggested a visit up the River Jordan, 70 kilometres or so through mountainous country, to its source. At that time, as now, merit attached to a journey to the source of a holy river. To accommodate the many pilgrims, Proconsul Hadrian had enhanced a village nearby, in the country of the Phillipians, but by naming it after the Roman Caesar he angered the Jews.

Around the source there have been through the ages small shrines or monuments to sacred figures, philosophers and wise men. At this stage the stature of Jesus had not yet been recognized, even by all the disciples. But looking round him we are told he asked whom he resembled. The replies of Peter and Matthew might have been prompted by the small shrines on either hand. However, Thomas had beheld him, with awe and wonder —incomparable. Immediately Jesus implied that in a certain sense the experience of Oneness made something common to both the disciple and to the Source. This was the event and the moment that established their twin-ship.

The source itself of the Jordan is a powerful spring that gushes, bubbling, out of the clefts in the rock at this place. The significance of the dialogue with Thomas that follows is heightened by the newness of the water of the spring, that this spring and the Jordan is the only river in Palestine that flows continuously throughout the year, and by the immense historical and spiritual importance of the Jordan to anyone born a Jew.

There then develops a situation of a type that is well authenticated in other situations: Jesus could discern the spiritual capability of a follower, and, taking him aside, gave a facet of Truth that others were not yet ready to grasp. We cannot tell what Jesus said. But it is very clear that Jesus taught his chosen disciple something that he and his colleagues considered to be blasphemous and punishable by ritual stoning, and had the power to set the world on fire. There is not much likelihood that the others would wish to record this. How could anyone other than he who had this daunting experience recount it, or feel it important to record it? It can only be the way Thomas put his authenticating 'signature' to his Gospel—for those with eyes to see it.

Turning to the Master

101
1. He who does not turn away from his father and his mother
2. in my way
3. will not be able to become my disciple;
4. and he who does not love his Father and his Mother
5. in my way
6. will not be able to become my disciple;
7. for my mother has begotten me
8. but my true Mother gave me <u>L</u>ife.

104
1. They said to him:
2. Come and let us pray today and let us fast!
3. Jesus said:
4. What therefore is the sin that I have committed
5. or in what have I been overcome?
6. But when the bridegroom comes forth from the bridal chamber
7. then let them fast and let them pray.

100

1. *They showed Jesus a gold coin*
2. *and said to him:*
3. *Caesar's agents demand taxes from us.*
4. *He said to them:*
5. *Give the things of Caesar to Caesar,*
6. *give the things of God to God,*
7. *and that which is mine, give to me.*

In turning to see Jesus it is of inestimable value—in fact it may be said to be essential—also to consider the incidents and episodes concerning Jesus narrated in the Gospels of the Bible. When working on the meaning, import or significance of these narrated episodes, the clue is to seek an answer to the question: From the reaction of the disciples or other persons what quality in Jesus did they see?

They showed Jesus a gold coin (logion 100)

is the only saying in this Gospel where there is mention of God as the word is used in the New Testament scriptures.

Here in phrases 5 to 7 is another hierarchical sequence of phrases, of increasing significance. Will you be willing to accept Jesus' order of priorities in your own spiritual life?

To Know and Metanoïa

3

1. Jesus said:
2. If those who guide your Being say to you:
3. "Behold the Kingdom is in the heaven,"
4. then the birds of the sky will precede you;
5. if they say to you: "It is in the sea,"
6. then the fish will precede you.
7. But the Kingdom is in your centre
8. and is about you.
9. When you Know your Selves
10. then you will be Known,
11. and you will be aware that you are
12. the sons of the Living Father.
13. But if you do not Know yourselves
14. then you are in poverty,
15. and you are the poverty.

5

1. Jesus said:
2. Know Him who is before your face,
3. and what is hidden from you shall be revealed to you:
4. for there is nothing hidden that shall not be manifest.

46

1. Jesus said:
2. From Adam until John the Baptist,
3. among the children begotten of women
4. there is none higher than John the Baptist,
5. such that his vision will be able to see Truth.
6. But I have said:
7. He who amongst you becomes as a child
8. shall Know the Kingdom,
9. and he shall be higher than John.

69

1. Jesus said:
2. Happy are they
3. who have been pursued in their heart.
4. It is they
5. who have Known the Father in Truth.
6. Happy are they who are hungry,
7. so that the belly of those who desire
    to see Truth shall be satisfied.

78

1. Jesus said:
2. Why did you come forth to the country?
3. To see a reed shaken by the wind
4/5. and to see a man clothed in soft garments?
6. See, your kings and your nobles;
7. these are clothed in soft garments,
8. and they will not be able to Know the Truth.

105

1. Jesus said:
2. He who knows the Father and the Mother,
3. will be beyond all worldly parentage.

91

1. They said to him:
2. Tell us who you are
3. so that we may believe in you.
4. He said to them:
5. You scrutinize the face of heaven and earth,
6. and him who is before you
7. you have not known,
8. and you know not how to probe this
  revelation.

28

1 Jesus said:
2 I stood boldly in the midst of the world
3 and I manifested to them in the flesh.
4 I found them all drunk;
5 I found none among them athirst,
6 and my soul was afflicted for the sons of men
7 because they are blind in their heart
8 and they do not see
9 that empty they came into the world
10 and that empty they seek to go out of the world again,
11 except that now they are drunk.
12 When they shake off their wine,
13 then they will transform their Knowing.

The verb 'to know' is the key word of this Teaching, it is one of the most frequently used words. It appears in three forms in the Coptic of the ancient 'Thomas' document, all of which translate in the dictionary as 'to know'. The word ⲥⲟⲩⲱⲛ is used consistently with the meaning of a profound certainty known at the depth of your being. It is as when you say "I know that I am myself and no-one else". It is rendered here with an initial capital letter.

When spelled ⲥⲟⲟⲩⲛ it is used in the Coptic with lesser significance. It is here rendered variously, as 'to realize', 'to recognize', 'to understand', or 'to know' as when you say "I know it is raining".

The third form ⲉⲓⲙⲉ is lighter still, and is rendered as 'to be aware', as when you say "I am aware that there are many religions in the world".

In *Tell us who you are* (logion 91)

there is, in phrase 3, the only occurrence in the whole Gospel of the word 'believe', and it is used by disciples from the Hebrew background. In this Teaching, Jesus never refers to the concept of belief, or of believing, or of believers, he always replaces that by knowing.

Likewise, nowhere in this Gospel does Jesus make any reference to faith, to having faith, or to being one of the faithful.

Instead, the key concept of the Teaching is to know—spiritual Truth being something that is found and known.

Our Western culture is riddled with beliefs and the concept of belief. Even politicians, when expounding their policies speak of believing in them. However you will find it very beneficial to go through the ideas and things you believe in—your own collection of beliefs   and replace each one by something you can Know for certain. To begin with, try to avoid saying "I believe . . .". Then those beliefs will merely fade away gradually, and you will come to live with the spiritual quality of certainty. You will be following the Master.

Metanoïa[17] used in the heading to this chapter is a double Greek word. The meta- part means to transform, as in our metamorphosis when a chrysalis transforms into a butterfly. However the second part is much more subtle and meaningful. As Jesus uses it in the 'Thomas' Gospel in the final phrase and word of:

. . . When they shake off their wine,
then they will transform their Knowing.

he is using it in the sense of the Coptic ⲥⲟⲩⲱⲛ, a very fundamental Knowing at the centre of your Being. This saying emphasizes that such metanoïa will transform men, and therefore also women, from spiritual blindness and drunkenness—which gravely afflicted Jesus—into those Knowing spiritual Light and Life.

Metanoïa is obviously profoundly important, even though Jesus uses the word only once in 'Thomas'. However it can be seen that the word itself was important for Jesus, for he uses it many times in the ancient Greek versions of the gospels of the Bible.

Unfortunately, it might almost be called a calamity, from the Middle Ages and still to this day metanoïa in the words of Jesus in the Bible has been mistranslated as 'to repent'.

It is almost impossible to avoid picking up the idea of Jesus, or Christ, as a saviour, which means saving you from sins—whether these be something inherent or merely shortcomings. Intimately related to this is the idea of repentance—to repent of your sins. That however is a corruption of the important word metanoïa which Jesus used. Much better is to change your viewpoint and perspective to give it the meaning of a transformation of your Knowing.

To Know for certain and the transforming nature of metanoïa are two of the teachings in the Gospel of Thomas that certainly will make a difference to your spiritual life.

Birth and Death

18
1. The disciples said to Jesus:
2. Tell us in what way our end will be.
3. Jesus said:
4. Have you therefore discerned the beginning
5. since you seek after the end?
6. For in the Place where the beginning is,
7. there will be the end.
8. Happy is he who will stand boldly at the beginning,
9. he shall Know the end,
10. and shall find Life independent of death.

BIRTH AND DEATH

19

1 *Jesus said:*
2/3 *Happy is he who already was before he is.*
4 *If you become my disciples*
5 *and hear my logia,*
6 *even these stones will minister to you.*
7 *For you have five trees in Paradise*
8 *which are unchanged in summer or winter*
9 *and their leaves do not fall away.*
10 *He who knows them*
11 *shall find life independent of death.*

Jesus answers a question about death by directing you to become aware of your beginning. This topic is put near the start of this book because it affects us all; also, the responses we are given are rather spectacularly different from much that is in the Bible and the doctrines of the Christian Church. However some concepts are covered later in this book, so it may be necessary to come back to these two sayings later.

At that stage, when you are ready, take into account that the sayings in this Gospel are a whole, at least in the mind of him who said them. So look elsewhere for the meaning of Jesus' reply.

BIRTH AND DEATH

Happy is he who already was   Logion 19, page 50

If they say to you: Where are you from   Logion 50, page 53

Happy are the monakhos and the chosen   Logion 49, page 101

The man old in days will not hesitate   Logion 4, page 73.

These sayings reiterate that in our beginning we came from the Light; it is inherent within us, and by seeing it we come to the Life in the here and now that is independent of the death of the body.

Thus to know rightly the beginning and the end leads to living in the present, and concern about death does not arise.

These two sayings (logia 18 and 19) deal with the happiness of knowing that your true identity exists throughout life. It is there at the beginning (logion 4 spoke of that) and extends to the end. However it is more than a continuity within time; more specifically the Real Self is independent of time.

Such Life is not merely immortal, but rather it is outside of the concept of time, and so is independent of death.

Phrases 2 and 3 of the second of these two sayings are a prompt to take you to an awareness of an even higher level than the previous one. Whereas that directed you to disregard the beginning and the end—a duality—this refers to finding what was and is as a Oneness. The sayings heard and known inwardly by the disciple make a happy man, to whom even stones will minister, the trees of completeness are changeless through the seasons, and he finds Life independent of death.

Light at the Centre

24
1. His disciples said:
2. Show us the Place where you are,
3. because it is necessary for us to seek after it.
4. He said to them:
5. He who has ears let him hear:
6. There is *Light*
7. at the centre of a man of Light,
8. and he illumines the whole world.
9. If he does not shine,
10. there is darkness.

33
1. Jesus said:
2. What you will hear in one ear
3. and in the other Ear,
4. that proclaim from your housetops.
5. For no one lights a lamp
6. and puts it under a bowl,
7. nor does he put it in a hidden place,

(33)
> but he sets it on the lamp stand
> 9 in order that everyone who goes in and comes out
> 10 may see its light.

50
1. Jesus said:
2. If they say to you:
3. "Where are you from?"
4. say to them:
5. "We came from the Light
6. there, where the Light was,
7. by itself.
8. It stood boldly
9. and manifested itself in their image."
10. If they say to you:
11. "Who are you?"
12/13. say: "We are his sons
14. and we are the chosen of the Living Father."
15. If they question you:
16. "What is the sign of your Father in you?"
17. say to them:
18. "It is a movement with a repose."

Finding the Light at the Centre

109
1. Jesus said:
2. The Kingdom is like a man
3. who owned in his field a hidden treasure,
4. it being unknown to him.
5. He bequeathed it to his son after he died.
6. The son not knowing of it,
7. took that field
8. and sold it.
9. And he who bought it, came.
10. While ploughing, he found the treasure;
11. he began to lend money at interest
12. to whomsoever he wished.

111

1. *Jesus said:*
2. *The heavens and the earth will roll back*
3. *before you,*
4. *and he who is living, from the Living,*
5. *shall see neither death nor fear,*
6. *because Jesus says this:*
7. *For him who finds his true Self*
8. *the world of objects is of no worth.*

10

1. *Jesus said:*
2. *I have cast fire upon the world,*
3. *and behold, I guard it*
4. *until it is ablaze.*

Quenching Ahamkāra *

58
1. *Jesus said:*
2. *Happy is the man who has toiled to lose ahamkāra,*
3. *he has found the Life.*

71
1. *Jesus said:*
2. *I will overturn this house,*
3. *and no one will be able to build it again.*

---

* Ahamkāra is the name given here to a concept that is strange to us; the concept is considered on pages 65 onwards. It is the concept, rather than its name, that is important because it is the key to unlock the meanings of this significant group of sayings, and many others. Without it, these sayings remain impossibly difficult.

Ahamkāra[18] is pronounced as four quick syllables, three with short-a as in apple, and one with long-ā as in English car.

37

1. His disciples said:
2. On which day will you be manifest to us
3. and on which day will we behold you?
4. Jesus said:
5. When you strip yourselves of your shame,
6. and take your garments
7. and put them under your feet
8. even as little children,
9. and you trample them;
10. then shall you behold the Son
11. of Him who is living,
12. and you shall not fear.

70

1. Jesus said:
2. When you bring forth that in yourselves,
3. this which is yours will save you;
4. if you do not have that in yourselves,
5. this which is not yours in you will kill you.

97

1. Jesus said:
2. The Kingdom of the Father is like a woman
3. who was carrying a jar full of flour
4. while walking on a long road;
5. the handle of the jar broke
6. the flour streamed out behind her on the road.
7. As she did not know it
8. she could not be troubled by it.
9. When she had reached her house
10. she put the jar on the ground;
11. she found it empty.

98

1. Jesus said:
2. The Kingdom of the Father is like a man
3. wishing to kill a giant.
4. He drew the sword in his house,
5. he struck it through the wall
6. in order to be assured that his hand would
                                      be confident.
7. Then he slew the giant.

35

1. Jesus said:
2. It is not possible
3. for one to enter the house of the strong man
4. and take it by force
5. unless he binds his hands;
6. then he will plunder his house.

103

1. Jesus said:
2. Happy is the man who knows
3. where and when the robbers will creep in;
4. so that he will arise
5. and gather his strength
6. and prepare for action
7. before they come.

QUENCHING AHAMKĀRA

21

1. Mary said to Jesus:
2. Whom do your disciples resemble?
3. He said:
4. They resemble small children
5. dwelling in a field
6. which is not theirs.
7. When the owners of the field come,
8. they will say
9. "Release to us our field."
10. They strip off their outward façade before them
11. to release it to them
12. and to give back their field to them.
13. For this reason I say:
14. If the owner of the house is aware
15. that the thief is coming,
16. he will stay awake before he comes
17. and will not allow the thief
18. to tunnel into his house of his Kingdom
19. to carry away his goods.
20. But you, already watch the world,
21. prepare for action with great strength
22. lest the robbers should find a way
23. to come to you;

(21)

²⁴ because the advantage that you expect,
²⁵ they will find.
²⁶ Let there be in your centre
²⁷ a man who is understanding!
²⁸ When the produce ripened
²⁹ he came in haste, his sickle in his hand,
³⁰ he reaped it.
³¹ He who has ears to hear let him hear!

61

1. Jesus said:
2. Two will rest there on a couch:
3. one will die, the other will live.
4. Salome said:
5. Who are you, man?
6. Is it even as he from the One
7. that you reclined on my couch
8. and ate at my table?
9. Jesus said to her:
10. I am He who is,
11. from Him who is the same;
12. what belongs to my Father was given to me.
13. Salome said: I myself am your disciple.
14. Jesus added: Because of that I say this:
15. When he is emptied
16. he will be filled with Light;
17. but when he is divided
18. he will be filled with darkness.

QUENCHING AHAMKĀRA

28
1. Jesus said:
2. I stood boldly in the midst of the world
3. and I manifested to them in the flesh.
4. I found them all drunk;
5. I found none among them athirst,
6. and my soul was afflicted for the sons of men
7. because they are blind in their heart
8. and they do not see
9. that empty they came into the world
10. and that empty they seek to go out of the world again,
11. except that now they are drunk.
12. When they shake off their wine,
13. then they will transform their Knowing.

10
1. Jesus said:
2. I have cast fire upon the world,
3. and behold, I guard it
4. until it is ablaze.

QUENCHING AHAMKĀRA

7
1. Jesus said:
2. Happy is the lion which the man will eat,
3. and the lion will become man;
4. and abominated is the man whom the lion will eat,
5. and the lion will become man.

42
1. Jesus said:
2. Become your Real Self, as ahamkāra passes away.

QUENCHING AHAMKĀRA

The inner meaning of this group of sayings, which is probably the most difficult in this Teaching, can only be grasped by an awareness of a concept that is virtually absent from Western thought, even though it is central to several Eastern spiritual teachings. It involves a spiritual Teaching at a very high level.

No European languages have a word for the concept, so it will be best to borrow an Eastern word—ahamkāra. Its meaning is the dominance of the body, and of the mind and its emotions. This dominance veils the Real Self that lies at a higher level, even though only latent or hidden within each person. The main spiritual work is to quench the power of ahamkāra, to quench this dominance. Then the Real Self becomes spontaneously and automatically known.

Surprisingly, however, our ordinary speech touches on this, but without its significance being noted. We say "my body", "my mind and thoughts", "my feelings and emotions". These phrases come entirely naturally to us; we know them to be valid without anyone having to convince us. The point is: who is it who can say "my"? It is the hidden Real Self.

The Real Self, the true Self are synonyms. So too are Reality, Truth, the Absolute, the Ultimate; and also terms used in 'Thomas'—the All, One, Unity, the Kingdom, Life, the Living, the Father, Kingdom of the Father, the Father and the Mother, Light, the Pure Spirit, Kingdom of the heavens—all these are as facets on the jewel that is this. The jewel itself is of course beyond the capability of any word or words to describe—words make up a part of it and a part cannot describe the whole.

Ahamkāra may go under other names, especially when rendered into English. In Sufi literature there is the tiny poem where, as the 'little self' it is contrasted with the Real Self:[18]

QUENCHING AHAMKĀRA

> Awhile, as wont may be,
> self I did claim;
> true Self I did not see,
> but heard its name.
> I, being self-confined,
> Self did not merit,
> till, leaving self behind,
> did Self inherit. *

Ahamkāra derives from the mind, the emotions, the body and outward material factors. Being egoistic or selfish, self-opinionated, self-assertive or competitive, possessive, proud, changeable or vacillating, distressed or sad, despairing or fearful, placing reliance on concepts or doctrines, are all manifestations of ahamkāra. Suffering, whether of the body or in the emotions, can only belong to ahamkāra—the significance of this cannot be overemphasized.

Happiness and bliss, joyousness, peace and repose and tranquillity, certainty and stability and assurance and steadiness, contentment, consideration and generosity, gratitude, love and compassion, beauty, reliance, strength and fearlessness and courage, knowledge, all belong to the realm of the Real Self.

Anything seen by the Real Self is an object. So the Real Self looks on—it may be said looks down on from a higher level—the entire material and objective world. That world is seen, the Real Self is the seer.

---

* Jalal al Din Rumi (1207 – 1273), one of the greatest Persian Sufi poets.

QUENCHING AHAMKĀRA

Each of us is born free of ahamkāra, one of the special attractions of any small child. With the passing of years ahamkāra develops its domination. It is a major part of the spiritual work to overcome this. Jesus' 'temptations in the desert' recorded in the Biblical gospels may be a crude reference to the final stages of Jesus quenching ahamkāra to reach the freedom from it that made him ready to start his Ministry to mankind. One could say that ahamkāra is everything that Jesus was free from. But strangely the gospels of the Bible make no further reference to this nor propound its value for us.

Ahamkāra is far more easily seen in other people than in oneself —one of its tricks. It may be of value to learn first to discern it in others, in the events and contacts of daily life, in order to be more prepared to detect it when it manifests within.

Thomas recorded many sayings in his Gospel that relate to ahamkāra. It may help you to consider these in sub-groups, as Jesus worked to convey to his hearers first one and then another aspect of this concept. Thus the first of these groups comprises:

Happy is the man who has toiled to quench ahamkāra,

(logion 58)

I will overturn this house   (logion 71)

When you strip yourselves of your shame   (logion 37)

When you bring forth that in yourselves   (logion 70)

Here Jesus is speaking succinctly of what has been written above. (In this Teaching 'house' refers to the Being or essence of a man or woman.)

QUENCHING AHAMKĀRA

However, the last two of those sayings are somewhat difficult, so it may be helpful to have rather liberal paraphrases, as follows:

His disciples said:
On which day will you be manifest to us
and on which day will we behold you?
The Master said:
When you strip yourselves of your pride and ostentation,
and take your outward façades
and treat them as nought
—even as do little children—
and, furthermore, scorn and discard them;
Then shall you behold the living Master,
and you shall not fear.

And for the second paraphrase:

The Master said:
When you bring forth that which is inherently within yourselves,
this which is yours will save you;
but if you do not acknowledge that within yourselves,
the invasive ahamkara will kill you, denying access to Truth.

QUENCHING AHAMKĀRA

. . . like a woman who was carrying a jar full of flour
(logion 97)

. . . like a man wishing to kill a giant (logion 98)

Two simple word-pictures related to situations of his day. These must have been addressed to Jewish hearers because of the use of the Kingdom of Heaven as the state to be reached by quenching the dominance of ahamkāra, whether gradually throughout life as some people achieve it or by some violent action, as occurs with others.

It is not possible for one to enter the house of the strong man
(logion 35)

. . . knows where and when the robbers will creep in
(logion 103)

Whom do your disciples resemble? (logion 21)

Here the invasive ahamkāra is likened to the strong forces within us that, like robbers or a thief, steal away our awareness of what is truly within us. This wily ahamkāra can appear in many different forms—as a strong man, as brigands, or making us live in a field not really ours. All this needs to be watched for, and demands your strength to guard against it.

Salome said: Who are you, man? (logion 61)

I stood boldly in the midst of the world (logion 28)

QUENCHING AHAMKĀRA

When Jesus stayed in Salome's home she, in her wonderment, came very near the limit of what a hostess might say, bordering on the impertinent. Jesus, however, was above being offended, and responded with words of great profundity.[19] These swept through her, and it is the contrast between the arrogance of phrase 5 and the simple humility of phrase 13 expressing her discipleship that reveals the sudden collapse of her ahamkāra. Her reward, later, was to be named Salome, 'the perfect one'. The enigmatic quality of what Jesus then said to her, speaking so he could be heard by the others, vanishes by understanding it as "When one is emptied of ahamkāra", with the consequence and value of being thus emptied, and thereby filled undividedly with Light.[20]

Likewise, in logion 28, Jesus was afflicted in his soul because men, in their spiritual blindness and drunkenness, do not see that they were born without ahamkāra and later seek to rid themselves of it. By finding that emptiness it will be the means to achieve metanoïa, to transform their deepest Knowing.

In effect, Jesus is saying that only when you empty yourself of ahamkāra will Spiritual Truth be known. Jesus, Thomas and great saints attained this. Thus it may be said that in your search for illumination, reading or more so hearing the words of such a person will be of special worth.

I have cast fire upon the world (logion 10)

Happy is the lion which the man will eat (logion 7)

One meaning, at least, of the first saying is a simple assertion that the fire brought by Jesus has the capacity to burn up ahamkāra.[21]

QUENCHING AHAMKĀRA

The second is one of the more difficult sayings. It is in the nature of a Zen koan, where phrase 4 being the inverse or reverse of phrase 2, our ordinary mental and logical approach would expect phrases 3 and 5 also to be reversed. But, these being identical, we are challenged to rise to a higher level. The clue lies in the awareness that the lion represents ahamkāra; the Living man has assimilated this, not been consumed by it. It may also be helpful to have a more expanded paraphrase, thus:

Happy are the primeval forces that the
    enlightened man will assimilate,
and they will be integrated and purified by the man;
but abominated is the ordinary man consumed by
    those forces,
and they will constitute that man.

Become your Real Self, as ahamkāra passes away.
(logion 42)

Jesus distills and crystalizes the very heart of his Teaching in this tiny saying—its brevity precludes all dross, as pure gold from the refiner's fire. Jesus might well have given this to his closest disciples as a mantra—perhaps you could use it.

In the original it comprises only three words, which can be literally translated 'Become yourselves, passing by.' However the meaning comes through better in the calligraphic form.

The intent is to prompt us—it is in the imperative—to disregard the things of the material world or of our minds and

QUENCHING AHAMKĀRA

emotions, to become unattached to them. Thus, for example, to do all the outward things of living without being a 'doer'; or when troubles beset us to let them pass by; or to allow the good and pleasing things to come to us without in any way claiming them. All such attachment, or being a doer, or claiming comes from ahamkāra. Letting the dominance of that go, each of us becomes our Real Self.

Oneness

8
1 And he said:
2 The Man is like a wise fisherman
3 who cast his net into the sea;
4 he drew it up from the sea full of small fish.
5 Amongst them,
6 he found one large and fine fish.
7 That wise fisherman, he cast all the small fish
      down to the bottom of the sea,
8 he chose the large fish without difficulty.
9 He who has ears to hear let him hear!

4
1 Jesus said:
2 The man old in days will not hesitate
3 to ask a little child of seven days
4 about the Place of Life,
5 and he will live;
6 for many who are first shall become last
7 and they shall be a single One.

48

1. Jesus said:
2. If two make peace with each other
3. in this single house,
4. they will say to the mountain
5. "Move away"
6. and it shall move.

106

1. Jesus said:
2. When you make the two One,
3. you will become Sons of man,
4. and if you say:
5. "Mountain, move away,"
6. it shall move.

22

1. Jesus saw children who were being suckled.
2. He said to his disciples:
3. These children who are being suckled are like
4. those who enter the Kingdom.
5. They said to him:
6. Shall we then, being children,
7. enter the Kingdom?
8. Jesus said to them:
9. When you make the two One,
10. and you make the inner as the outer,
11. and the outer as the inner,
12. and the above as the below,
13. so that you will make the male and the female
14. into a single One,
15. in order that the male is not made male
16. nor the female made female;
17. when you make eyes into an eye,
18. and a hand into a hand,
19. and a foot into a foot,
20. and even an image into an image,
21. then shall you enter the Kingdom.

11

1. Jesus said:
2. This heaven will pass away,
3. and that which is above it will pass away,
4. and the dead do not live,
5. and the living will not die.
6. In the days you fed on what is dead,
7. you made of that, the living.
8. When you are in the light
9. what will you do!
10. On the day you were One,
11. you created the two;
12. but then being two,
13. what will you do?

ONENESS

87

1. Jesus said:
2. Wretched is the body that depends on a body,
3. and wretched is the soul that depends on these two.

112

1. Jesus said:
2. Woe to the flesh that depends upon the soul!
3. Woe to the soul that depends upon the flesh!

88

1. Jesus said:
2. The angels with the prophets will come to you
3. and they will give you what is yours.
4. You also, give what is in your hands
5. to them,
6. and say to yourselves:
7. On which day will they come
8. and receive what is theirs?

89

1. Jesus said:
2. Why do you wash the outside of the cup?
3. Do you not understand
4. that He who made the inside
5. is also He who made the outside.

30

1. Jesus said:
2. The place where there are three gods,
3. they are gods;
4. where there are two or one,
5. I myself am with him.

23

1. Jesus said:
2. I will choose you, one out of a thousand,
3. and two out of ten thousand,
4. and they shall stand boldly being a single One.

72

1. A man said to him:
2. Tell my brothers
3. to divide my father's possessions with me.
4. He said to him:
5. Oh man, who made me a divider?
6. He turned to his disciples,
7. he said to them:
8. Is it that I am a divider?

76

1. Jesus said:
2. The Kingdom of the Father is like a man, a merchant,
3. who owned merchandise,
4. and found a pearl.
5. That merchant was wise:
6. he sold the merchandise,
7. he bought this one single pearl for himself.
8. You also, seek after the treasure
9. which does not perish,
10. which remains in the place
11. where no moth comes near to devour,
12. and no worm destroys.

67

1. Jesus said:
2. He who understands the All,
3. but is lacking himself
4. lacks everything.

62

1. Jesus said:
2. I tell my mysteries
3. to those who are worthy of my mysteries.
4. Whatever your right hand will do,
5. let not your left hand be aware
6. of what it does.

77

1. Jesus said:
2. I am the Light that is above all things.
3. I am the All.
4. The All comes forth from me,
5. and the All extends throughout me.
6. Cleave the wood, I am there;
7. raise the stone,
8. and you shall find me there.

ONENESS

The teaching about Oneness lies at the centre and heart of the Gospel of Thomas. Jesus spoke many times in various ways about the One or the All. These terms are in the Greek idiom, and must have been used when he was amongst the Hellenist people. It is not difficult to see that they refer to the same thing—more strictly they both point to the same Place; either of them has to be complete, and there can only be one completeness.

Referring to this teaching as Oneness, at the highest level it becomes Spiritual Truth or Ultimate Reality. This group of sayings direct you to recognize that whenever in the spiritual a duality, a pair, is noted, with further seeking an underlying unity or over-riding Oneness may be found. To many this truism may be first experienced when a man and woman wed, and find the Oneness of marriage.

The man old in days will not hesitate   (logion 4)

Not with the mind could you accept that an old man might see the essence of Life in an infant. But by going to a deeper Place within us the wonder, still unsullied, inherent within each person may be discerned.

If two make peace with each other   (logion 48)

When you make the two One,   (logion 106)

The mountain in these two sayings is that of distress and suffering, which can only belong to the realm of ahamkāra. The two refers to ahamkāra and the Real Self. The only way ahamkāra and the Real Self can make peace with each other within your Being, or the two be made One, is for ahamkāra to be quenched. Then the Real Self, which may be said to reside within the body and mind but not be of either, can reign alone.

Here Jesus asserts his Teaching, perhaps of paramount consequence to each man or woman in going through life, that when emptied of ahamkāra the mountain of suffering shall—it is a promise and a command—move away. His is the same objective as Buddha's, the release from suffering, even if he reaches it by a different route.

Jesus saw children who were being suckled (logion 22)

is developed into one of the great sayings by Jesus about Oneness, where he reiterates examples of the basic point he is making. It is a saying worth returning to, even over a period of years.

It starts with simple questions, where Jesus was amongst Jewish people, accustomed to the Aramaic idiom, who had at least discerned the unsullied quality in each of us as children. He responds in characteristically Semitic speech, yet by phrase 9 it has become necessary to move to the Greek idiom to provide the answers. Amongst the many instances of two becoming One, Unity found from duality, that in phrase 9 refers—as so often in this Teaching—to ahamkāra and the Self within each of us.

By phrase 14 maleness and femaleness have merged, or risen to a level for which we have the word mankind. This is amplified or confirmed in phrases 15 and 16, where both the male and the female have disappeared.

ONENESS

In phrase 17 Jesus refers, in symbolic style, to your pair of physical eyes being transformed into a single spiritual eye with which you may discern spiritual Truth.

He goes on in the following phrases to emphasize that all aspects of the body—the hand, the foot and even the image within—are to be transformed into the single spiritual quality that lies within. Finally Jesus takes you back to the Jewish idiom

This heaven will pass away   (logion 11)

For this logion you will be helped by a very liberally-worded paraphrase:

Everything above, being of the world of objects, will pass away.

The dead, being in duality, do not live,

the living, in the Unity, will not die.

In the days when you fed on the world of objects you made it alive.

When you come into the Light, what will you do?

On the day you were One you made it duality,

but then being two, what will you do?

This relates to the Teaching that each of us is originally a Oneness, has developed a duality—largely through the concepts and doctrines of the mind—can come back to the Unity during our life in this world, in which there is no death, and can then purify whatever we assimilate. This can be done by answer to the question: What will you do? It is a quest by the individual..

Spiritual Life Essential

40
1. *Jesus said:*
2. *A vine was planted without the Father*
3. *and being not made firm,*
4. *it will be pulled up by its roots*
5. *and perish.*

41
1. *Jesus said:*
2. *He who has in his hand,*
3. *to him shall be given;*
4. *and he who does not have,*
5. *even the little that he has*
6. *shall be taken from him.*

45

1. Jesus said:
2. Grapes are not harvested from thorn trees
3. nor are figs gathered from thistles,
4. for these give no fruit.
5. A good man brings forth good from his storehouse,
6. a bad man brings forth ill
7. from his wicked storehouse
8. which is in his heart,
9. and he speaks ill:
10. for out of the abundance of the heart
11. he brings forth ill.

44

1. Jesus said:
2. He who blasphemes against the Father,
3. it shall be forgiven him,
4. and he who blasphemes against the Son,
5. it shall be forgiven him;
6. but he who blasphemes against the pure Spirit,
7. it shall not be forgiven him, neither on earth nor in heaven.

From Small Things Great Grow

9
1. Jesus said:
2. Behold, the sower went out.
3. He filled his hand and threw.
4. Some seeds indeed fell on the road;
5. the birds came and plundered them.
6. Others fell on the rock
7. and did not take root in the earth
8. nor did they send up their heads to the sky.
9. And others fell on thorn trees;
10. these choked the seeds
11. and the worms ate them.
12. Others fell on tilled earth,
13. which brought forth good produce to the sky;
14. it bore sixty per measure
15. even one hundred and twenty per measure.

20

1. The disciples said to Jesus:
2. Tell us, what is the Kingdom of the heavens like?
3. He said to them:
4. It is like a grain of mustard,
5. smaller than all seeds;
6. but when it falls on the tilled earth,
7. it sends forth a large stem
8. and becomes a shelter for the birds of the sky.

96

1. Jesus said:
2. The Kingdom of the Father is like a woman,
3. who took a little leaven,
4. hid it in dough
5. and of it made large loaves.
6. He who has ears let him hear!

The final part of

Behold, the sower went out (logion 9)

tells us that only a person who earnestly seeks the words of Jesus, and who has the urge to open the heart to his presence within, will thereby prepare the tilled earth in which they will grow a hundredfold.

The Way to the Kingdom

94
1. Jesus said:
2. He who seeks shall find,
3. and to him who knocks it shall be opened.

54
1. Jesus said:
2. Happy are the poor,
3. for yours is the Kingdom of the heavens.

6
1. His disciples questioned, they said to him:
2. Do you wish that we should fast?
3. And in which way should we pray?
4. Should we give alms?
5. and what diet should we observe?
6. Jesus said:

(6)
7 Do not lie,
8 and do not do what you dislike,
9 for all things are revealed before heaven.
10 For there is nothing hidden that shall not be manifest,
11 and there is nothing concealed
12 that shall remain without being revealed.

99
1 The disciples said to him:
2 Your brothers and your mother are standing outside.
3 He said to them:
4 Those here who do the wish of my Father
5 they are my brothers and my mother.
6 These are they
7 who shall enter the Kingdom of my Father.

12

1. The disciples said to Jesus:
2. We realize that you will go away from us;
3. who is it that will be great over us?
4. Jesus said to them:
5. Whatever place you have come to,
6. you will go to James the righteous,
7. because of whom heaven and earth came into being.

78

1. Jesus said:
2. Why did you come forth to the country?
3. To see a reed shaken by the wind
4/5. and to see a man clothed in soft garments?
6. See, your kings and your nobles;
7. these are clothed in soft garments,
8. and they will not be able to Know the Truth.

81

1. Jesus said:
2. He who has become spiritually rich,
3. let him become king;
4. and he who has temporal power,
5. let him renounce it!

57

1. Jesus said:
2. The Kingdom of the Father is like a man
3. who owned good seed.
4. His enemy came by night,
5. he sowed weeds among the good seed.
6. The man did not allow the labourers to pull up the weeds;
7. he said to them: lest perhaps you should go,
8. saying "we will pull up the weeds,"
9. and you pull up the wheat with it.
10. For on the day of the harvest
11. the weeds will appear;
12. they will be pulled up and will be burned.

64
1. Jesus said:
2. A man had guests
3. and when he had prepared the dinner
4. he sent his servant to invite the guests.
5. He went to the first
6. and said to him:
7. "My master invites you."
8. He said:
9. "I have some money for some traders;
10. they will come to me in the evening,
11. I will go and place orders with them.
12. I ask to be excused from the dinner."
13. He went to another
14. he said to him:
15. "My master invites you."
16. He said to him:
17. "I have bought a house and they request me for a day.
18. I will not be available."
19. He came to another
20. he said to him:
21. "My master invites you."
22. He said to him:

(64)

23 "My friend is to be married
24 and I am to arrange a feast;
25 I shall not be able to come.
26 I ask to be excused from the dinner."
27 He went to another
28 he said to him:
29 "My master invites you."
30 He said to him:
31 "I have bought a farm,
32 I go to collect the rent
33 I shall not be able to come,
34 I ask to be excused."
35 The servant came;
36 he said to his master:
37 "Those whom you have invited to the dinner
have excused themselves."
38 The master said to his servant
39 "Go outside to the roads,
40 bring those whom you will find,
41 so that they may dine."
42 Those preoccupied with material concerns
43 shall not enter
44 the Place of my Father.

85
1. Jesus said:
2. Adam came into being from a great power
3. and a great richness,
4. and he was not worthy of you;
5. for had he been worthy,
6. he would not have tasted death.

110
1. Jesus said:
2. He who has found the world
3. and become rich,
4. let him deny the world!

You may well be attracted by a Teaching on 'The Way' for which many sayings are included in 'Thomas'. When looked on as a whole, they are unusual in seeming to have a certain negativeness. On closer consideration however it may be seen that the negative tone applies to material or objective qualities. Thus it becomes clear that Jesus was working to dispel those—even though they so readily come to mind—because essentially they all belong to the realm of ahamkāra.

This is well shown in the long story of the feast

A man had guests (logion 64)

which in its outward form refers to preoccupation with worldly affairs. Yet inwardly it is also about the many excuses arising from ahamkāra that it is all too easy to find for not accepting 'the call' or, more dangerously, ignoring it.

Nevertheless discrimination needs to be applied. For if

Why did you come forth to the country (logion 78)

were to be regarded as a call to the life of an ascetic it would only be to see the first level of meaning. It is the final phrase that directs you towards non-attachment to worldly things.

In *We realize that you will go away from us* (logion 12)

this dialogue refers to James, one of the blood brothers of Jesus, who came in due course to take a leading part amongst the group of disciples of Jewish background—not yet a Church—that became established in Jerusalem. The final phrase is one that would have been familiar to his Jewish hearers.

Spiritual Richness

63
1. Jesus said:
2. There was a rich man
3. who had much wealth.
4. He said:
5. I will use my wealth
6. in order that I may sow and reap and plant,
7. and fill my storehouses with produce
8. so that I lack nothing.
9. This was what he thought in his heart;
10. and during that night he died.
11. He who has ears let him hear!

60

1. They saw a Samaritan,
2. carrying a lamb,
3. going into Judea.
4. He said to his disciples:
5. Why does this man carry the lamb around?
6. They said to him:
7. In order that he may kill it and eat it.
8. He said to them:
9. As long as it is alive
10. he will not eat it,
11. but only if he kills it
12. and it becomes a corpse.
13. They said:
14. Otherwise he will not be able to do it.
15. He said to them:
16. You yourselves, seek after a Place for yourselves
17. within Repose,
18. lest you become corpses
19. and be eaten.

90
1 Jesus said:
2 Come to me,
3 for easy is my yoke
4 and my lordship is gentle,
5 and you shall find Repose for yourselves.

51
1 His disciples said to him:
2 On which day
3 will the repose of the dead come about?
4 And on which day
5 will the new world come?
6 He said to them:
7 What you expect has come
8 but you, you recognize it not.

113

1. His disciples said to him:
2. On which day will the Kingdom come?
3. Jesus said: It will not come by expectation.
4. They will not say:
5. "Behold, it is here!"
6. or "Behold, there!"
7. But the Kingdom of the Father is spread out over the earth
8. and men do not see it.

There was a rich man (Logion 63)

is clearly a warning against the abuse of knowledge—filling the internal storehouses—and boasting of it. This could result in spiritual pride.

Come to me, for easy is my yoke (Logion 90)

The meaning underlying the word 'yoke' is a joining together. Here the joining to Jesus leads to a special kind of Repose.

On which day will the repose of the dead come about? (Logion 51)

A cardinal feature of this Teaching is that the true Life can be found and known during this life, rather than being only in some life after death or in a messianic future or at the millennium.

Monakhos and Courage

16
1. Jesus said:
2. 'Perhaps men think that I have come
3. to cast concord upon the earth;
4. they do not realize that perhaps my coming
5. will cast separations upon the earth;
6. even fire, sword, strife!
7. For there may be five in a home,
8. three will be against two,
9. and two against three,
10. the father against the son,
11. and the son against the father;
12. then they shall stand boldly, being monakhos.

49
1. Jesus said:
2. Happy are the monakhos and the chosen
3. for you shall find the Kingdom.
4. Because you are from the heart of it,
5. you shall return there again.

75

1. *Jesus said:*
2/3. *There are many standing at the door,*
4. *but the monakhos are they*
5. *who shall enter the marriage place.*

55

1. *Jesus said:*
2. *He who does not turn away from his father and his mother*
3. *will not be able to become my disciple,*
4. *and he who does not turn away from his brothers and sisters*
5. *and does not bear his cares in my way,*
6. *will not be worthy of me.*

Three times in 'Thomas' Jesus employs the rarely used Greek word *monakhos*. It does not translate into English. The nearest is the rather unsatisfactory word 'loner', in the sense of the nineteenth century American phrase "Go west, young man". In South Africa then they were called Pioneers, and were whole families. It implies foremost an independence, with perhaps something of an adventure about it. It means one who is willing to go forward on his own, who can become detached as a liner loosens its moorings to set out on a voyage.

In *Perhaps men think that I have come* (logion 16)

the Coptic word in phrase 5 carries a sense of a positive type of division, a discrimination. Further, to stand boldly as a monakhos requires a certain sort of Courage; with a kind of determination and resolution. To walk your spiritual life with independence, and without going with the herd, whether that be in the community or within the family. It is because what Jesus came for was new, something different. That Courage resides in and comes from the Real Self.

In *Happy are the monakhos and the chosen* (logion 49)

in the Coptic the word 'chosen' carries the sense of being separated rather than being favoured.

He who does not turn away from his father and mother

(logion 55)

To 'turn away from' is a rather free rendering of the Greek word *miseo* in phrases 2 and 5, which has no English equivalent to give its right flavour; it is a contrast with 'to love', for which we would need to invent a word 'to dis-love'.

However, here and in logion 101 (page 49), the inner meaning is 'to detach from', a separation of the psyche, as given more specifically in the following paraphrase:

He who does not free himself from attachment to his
father and his mother
will not be able to become my disciple,
and he who does not free himself from his brothers and sisters
and does not have my sort of Courage,
will not be worthy of me.

This word, and the Greek word monakhos, and also the more recent term 'non-attachment', all point to the same concept. Specifically, in this saying, 'father, mother, brothers, sisters' may be applied to the religion of your family or upbringing. It might also apply to what you may have subsequently picked up from a religion that does not satisfy you.

Happiness

68
1. Jesus said:
2. Happy are you
3. when you are disliked
4. and you are pursued;
5. and no Place will be found there,
6. where you have been pursued in the heart.

69
1. Jesus said:
2. Happy are they
3. who have been pursued in their heart.
4. It is they
5. who have known the Father in Truth.
6. Happy are they who are hungry,
7. so that the belly of those who desire
        to see Truth shall be satisfied.

54

1. Jesus said:
2. Happy are the poor,
3. for yours is the Kingdom of the heavens.

58

1. Jesus said:
2. Happy is the man who has toiled to lose ahamkāra,
3. he has found the Life.

103

1. Jesus said:
2. Happy is the man who knows
3. where and when the robbers will creep in;
4. so that he will arise
5. and gather his strength
6. and prepare for action
7. before they come.

7

1. Jesus said:
2. Happy is the lion which the man will eat,
3. and the lion will become man;
4. and abominated is the man whom the lion will eat,
5. and the lion will become man.

18

1. The disciples said to Jesus:
2. Tell us in what way our end will be.
3. Jesus said:
4. Have you therefore discerned the beginning
5. since you seek after the end?
6. For in the Place where the beginning is,
7. there will be the end.
8. Happy is he who will stand boldly at the beginning,
9. he shall Know the end,
10. and shall find Life independent of death.

19

1. Jesus said:
2/3. Happy is he who already was before he is.
4. If you become my disciples
5. and hear my logia,
6. even these stones will minister to you.
7. For you have five trees in Paradise
8. which are unchanged in summer or winter
9. and their leaves do not fall away.
10. He who Knows them
11. shall find Life independent of death.

49

1. Jesus said:
2. Happy are the monakhos and the chosen
3. for you shall find the Kingdom.
4. Because you are from the heart of it,
5. you shall return there again.

90

1. Jesus said:
2. Come to me,
3. for easy is my yoke
4. and my lordship is gentle,
5. and you shall find Repose for yourselves.

HAPPINESS

The ten sayings in which Jesus refers to Happiness have been grouped together to emphasize that this is one of the themes he spoke of most frequently, using the Greek word makarios.[22] The only key-words used more frequently in 'Thomas' are the Kingdom, to find, to Know, the living and the Light.

It is apparent that the sayings of Jesus with makarios must have been given on many different occasions, as prompted by the opportunity or situation. Can you allow yourself to visualize Jesus going about with his disciples carrying an aura about him that led to his frequent use of this word?

Even so, happiness and to be happy in English may not immediately carry the intended meaning. It is not so much merriment as joy or bliss, associated with a profound contentment that leads to a repose. It is therefore convenient to invent a compound word happiness-or-bliss. A similar name is joyousness. It does not appear so much as laughter (although it may come as a great challenge to us to visualize Jesus laughing with his disciples) but as a poise and radiance. It is derived not from a response to external events but comes from a condition or state of being within. It may be regarded as a flowering of the Self, so that any of the sayings 'Happy is he who does so-and-so' is a pointer towards coming to an awareness of the true centre that lies within.

Thus this emphasis, both here and in the sayings of Jesus, stems directly from Happiness being one of the facets of the jewel that comprises spiritual Truth.

Images

22

1. Jesus saw children who were being suckled.
2. He said to his disciples:
3. These children who are being suckled are like
4. those who enter the Kingdom.
5. They said to him:
6. Shall we then, being children,
7. enter the Kingdom?
8. Jesus said to them:
9. When you make the two One,
10. and you make the inner as the outer,
11. and the outer as the inner,
12. and the above as the below,
13. so that you will make the male and the female
14. into a single One,
15. in order that the male is not made male
16. nor the female made female;
17. when you make eyes into an eye,
18. and a hand into a hand,
19. and a foot into a foot,
20. and even an image into an image,
21. then shall you enter the Kingdom.

50

1. Jesus said:
2. If they say to you:
3. "Where are you from?"
4. say to them:
5. "We came from the Light
6. there, where the Light was,
7. by itself.
8. It stood boldly
9. and manifested itself in their image."
10. If they say to you:
11. "Who are you?"
12/13. say: "We are his sons
14. and we are the chosen of the Living Father."
15. If they question you:
16. "What is the sign of your Father in you?"
17. say to them:
18. "It is a movement with a repose."

83

1. Jesus said:
2. The images are manifest to man
3. and the light that is amongst them is hidden.
4. In the image of the Light of the Father
5. the Light will reveal itself
6. and his image is hidden by his Light.

84

1. Jesus said:
2. In the days you see your resemblance,
3. you rejoice.
4. But when you will see your images
5. that in the beginning were in you,
6. which neither die nor are manifest,
7. oh! how will you bear the revelation!

IMAGES

These are the four sayings whereby Jesus prompts you to explore his highly evolved concept of Images. There must have been some of his disciples, devotedly following him with their lives changed, who had not risen to the level of this concept. So it may be for some today; yet that awareness may come with the passage of several years.

The word used in 'Thomas' is the Greek *eikon* from which we get icon. An image may be thought of as being like a casting derived from a pattern; it is an exact replica, not the original, nor is it a reproduction. An icon is not a representation. Michelangelo gave us on the ceiling of the Sistine Chapel the greatest visual representation of God, to convey symbolically by the touch of fingers the passing of divine quality into man. An icon of the Eastern Orthodox Church is different. It is an exact copy, but not the original, of a form invested with spiritual significance. The artist who paints each particular icon serves a long training under a master, and makes a copy that retains all the qualities of the original, thereby conveying the symbolism unsullied.

The wonderful saying

Jesus saw children being suckled (logion 22)

which we have already had occasion to consider, comprises a hierarchical series of phrases each one contrasting a spiritual form with a mental or material form. So when image occurs as the penultimate phrase it is prompting you to find the spiritual meaning of 'icon'.

Note furthermore that image occurs as the last of the four phrases 17 to 20 where you are being invited to go with Jesus into a region that is beyond mental processes. It is a concept beyond

IMAGES

even the spiritual eye, the hand or the foot, up in a region of its own.

So in the first of these sayings you are being led to find a spiritual form of something that previously may have been a mental idea; to rise to the spiritual level above a mere thought-form. It is one of the gateways into the Kingdom.

In phrases 5 to 9 of:

If they say to you "Where are you from?" (logion 50)

the two sentences speak of our coming from the self-existing Light; we saw this in the baby, and hence in ourselves. But in the third phrase you are suddenly taken to a very much higher level. The Light manifested itself in their image. 'Their' relates to 'we', these are the only plural words in the saying. So, however startling it may seem, we are being told the Light is the image of ourselves. The original is the highest in mankind, the Light is its replica, its emanation.

The images are manifest to man (logion 83)

starts with the mental images we make but, because they come from ahamkāra—of which the ordinary mind is a part—the light within them is hidden. However, the Light of the Father is the true Light and, as we find that, the true Light reveals itself. So far, so good. However, you need to look at the third phrase more closely. It is not saying the image of the Father, such as in the idea we might have of 'man being made in the image of God'. It is the first part of a longer expression that spans over three phrases. In the last of those 'his image is hidden' is a way of saying the Father is imageless, he is the original. And so his imageless nature is hidden by his Light. This is the same as where we can say 'the light reveals', and 'the brilliance of the light conceals'. Yet we have also been told that the Light is the image of man. So this is a paradox of the conjunction of opposites, for the grasping of which it is necessary to get beyond the words and the mind—to get into the experience of Oneness which usually can only be found in contemplation. Here we have an instance of a description of the indescribable, a definition of the indefinable, an expression of the inexpressible. This is a *via media* attempting to convey something that cannot be expressed in language, but only experienced.

The days you see your resemblance, (logion 84)

This saying is a complement to the preceding one. In its first phrase it reminds us of the rejoicing we feel as we recognize that what is at our Centre resembles the Light. Then, going on, we come to see that this image was pre-existent, it does not need to manifest itself because it was always there, and it is not affected by our death. Put another way, the image of the Light within us is eternal, not in the sense that it goes on for ever but in the much more profound sense that it is independent of time. It is just in this way that by finding the inner meaning of these sayings you will find Life that is independent of death. This, indeed, can be a revelation that is almost overwhelming.

Old Order and New Way

34
1. Jesus said:
2. If a blind man guides the Being of a blind man,
3. both of them fall to the bottom of a pit.

46
1. Jesus said:
2. From Adam until John the Baptist,
3. among the children begotten of women
4. there is none higher than John the Baptist,
5. such that his vision will be able to see Truth.
6. But I have said:
7. He who amongst you becomes as a child
8. shall Know the Kingdom,
9. and he shall be higher than John.

52

1. His disciples said to him:
2. Twenty-four prophets spoke in Israel
3. and they all spoke about your nature.
4. He said to them:
5. You have ignored Him who is living before you
6. and you have spoken about the dead.

39

1. Jesus said:
2. The Pharisees and the scribes
3. took the keys of Knowledge,
4. and they hid them.
5. Neither did they enter,
6. nor did they allow
7. those who wished to enter.
8. But you, become prudent as serpents
9. and innocent even as doves.

102

1. Jesus said:
2. Woe to them, the Pharisees!
3. For they resemble a dog
4. sleeping in the oxen's manger;
5. for neither does he eat
6. nor does he allow the oxen to eat.

43

1. His disciples said to him:
2. Who are you that you should say these things to us?
3. [Jesus said to them:] From what I say to you,
4. are you not aware who I am?
5. But you, you were even as the Jews:
6. for they love the tree,
7. they dislike its fruit;
8. and they love the fruit,
9. they dislike the tree.

53

1. His disciples said to him:
2. Is circumcision beneficial or not?
3. He said to them:
4. If it were beneficial,
5. their father would beget them circumcised from their mother.
6. But the loss of ahamkāra
7. gives the ultimate benefit.

47

1. Jesus said:
2. It is impossible
3. for a man to mount two horses,
4. for him to stretch two bows;
5. and it is impossible
6. for a servant to serve two masters,
7. otherwise he will honour the one
8. and offend the other.
9. Let a man drink old wine
10. and now he wants to drink new wine.
11. And new wine is not poured
12. into old wineskins,
13. lest they should burst;
14. and old wine is not poured
15. into a new wineskin,
16. lest this be spoiled.
17. An old patch is not sewn
18. on to a new garment,
19. because there would be a division.

Something new is an emphatic theme of the Gospel of Thomas. That is to say, in these sayings of Jesus he was asserting that what he was presenting was new. It was not just an advance, a development or progression of what was before, but was a new departure for those who heard and saw him inwardly.

Twenty-four prophets spoke in Israel (Logion 52)

Jesus contrasts the views of the disciples, that the revelations of the Prophets are what is significant, with the living word he is giving them.

It is impossible for a man to mount two horses (Logion 47)

is the most telling on this theme, if only because of the impact of the reiteration of very simple everyday situations familiar to people who came chiefly from the countryside. Seven word-pictures are given as a coherent series, all emphasizing the same point and building up the impact.

In those days old wine, stored in wineskins, was stale wine. The division, as the word is used in phrase 19, of a garment could be called a rent.

The gospels of the Bible tell of two occasions when Jesus spoke to the four- or the five-thousand. What he gave them was sustenance, so 'all were satisfied'. Perhaps inaudible to some of them, they could see him with both their outer eyes and their inner eye. With that, they saw something new, and it was satisfying.

We cannot see Jesus with our outer eyes. But let yours dwell on a copy, the best that can be obtained, of his radiant living form portrayed in an icon of the Eastern Orthodox Church. Let this be put in some special place of your home. Let living flowers be always kept beside it. Spend some minutes of every day before it, gazing intently. Then your inner eye may come to see him. There will be something new, and it too will be satisfying.

Beyond Femininity

114

1. *Simon Peter said to them:*
2. *Let Mary go out from amongst us,*
3. *because women are not worthy of the Life.*
4. *Jesus said:*
5. *Behold, I will guide her Being,*
6. *in order that I make her male*
7/8. *that she, like you, shall become a living spirit.*
9. *For every person who transcends being woman or man*
10. *shall enter the Kingdom of the heavens.*

22

1. *Jesus saw children who were being suckled.*
2. *He said to his disciples:*
3. *These children who are being suckled are like*
4. *those who enter the Kingdom.*
5. *They said to him:*
6. *Shall we then, being children,*
7. *enter the Kingdom?*
8. *Jesus said to them:*
9. *When you make the two One,*
10. *and you make the inner as the outer,*
11. *and the outer as the inner,*
12. *and the above as the below,*
13. *so that you will make the male and the female*
14. *into a single One,*
15. *in order that the male is not made male*
16. *nor the female made female;*
17. *when you make eyes into an eye,*
18. *and a hand into a hand,*
19. *and a foot into a foot,*
20. *and even an image into an image,*
21. *then shall you enter the Kingdom.*

BEYOND FEMININITY

101
1. He who does not turn away from his father and his mother
2. in my way
3. will not be able to become my disciple;
4. and he who does not love his Father and his Mother
5. in my way
6. will not be able to become my disciple;
7. for my mother has begotten me
8. but my true Mother gave me Life.

105
1. Jesus said:
2. He who knows the Father and the Mother,
3. will be beyond all worldly parentage.

Masculinity and femininity are a duality. Jesus urges us to go beyond that, to rise to something higher. His aim is to teach us to experience Oneness.

Wealth in Poverty

29
1. *Jesus said:*
2. *If the flesh has come into being because of the spirit,*
3. *it is a marvel;*
4. *but if the spirit has come into being because of the body,*
5. *it is a marvel of marvels.*
6. *But I, I marvel at this:*
7. *about this great richness of spiritual Truth*
8. *put within this poor world of objects.*

Simplicity of Living

27
1 *If you transcend not the world of objects,*
2 *you will not find the Kingdom;*
3 *if you keep not the sabbath as a true sabbath,*
4 *you will not behold the Father.*

56
1 *Jesus said:*
2 *He who has known the world,*
3 *has found a corpse;*
4 *and he who has found a corpse*
5 *of him the world is not worthy.*

80
1 *Jesus said:*
2 *He who has known the world*
3 *has found the body;*
4 *but he who has found the body*
5 *of him the world is not worthy.*

SIMPLICITY OF LIVING

It is easy to imagine that as Jesus walked about his country, staying where he could, he had a simple way of living. At least the evidence is that he turned his back on luxury, ostentation and all intemperance. Thomas, accompanying him, would have shared this.

Certainly these sayings are compatible with those of other spiritual Teachers, as they urge their followers to forego those indulgences that are attractive to the body and the physical senses, material concerns that only serve to feed ahamkāra. It is an essential preliminary in the training of every Tibetan Buddhist monk. In the West the Quaker community, and there are others, practice such simplicity, in an easy undogmatic manner, and find it very rewarding, a kind of release. On the other hand, discrimination is needed to distinguish between such cleansing of your material life and any abnegation or asceticism. That emphasis would merely lead back to the realm of ahamkāra in a negative sense.

It is not possible to tell why Thomas repeated two of these sayings, differing only in a single Greek word *ptōma* a corpse and *sōma* a body—no other saying is repeated. They occur quite widely separated in the original manuscript, and the most simple explanation is that while dictating to the scribe Thomas merely forgot that he had recorded the saying once already.

Jesus' Disappointment

31
1. *Jesus said:*
2. *No prophet is accepted in his own village;*
3. *no physician heals those who recognize him.*

74
1. *He said:*
2. *Lord, there are many around the well*
3. *but none in the well.*

73
1. *Jesus said:*
2. *The harvest is indeed great,*
3. *but the labourers are few.*
4. *Entreat, therefore, the Lord*
5. *to send labourers to the harvest.*

JESUS' DISAPPOINTMENT

92
1 Jesus said:
2 Seek and you will find.
3 But those things
4 that you asked me in those days
5 I did not tell you then;
6 now I desire to tell them
7 but you do not seek after them.

91
1 They said to him:
2 Tell us who you are
3 so that we may believe in you.
4 He said to them:
5 You scrutinize the face of heaven and earth,
6 and him who is before you
7 you have not known,
8 and you know not how to probe this
                                      revelation.

JESUS' DISAPPOINTMENT

38
1. Jesus said:
2. Many times have you longed to hear these logia
3. which I say to you,
4. and you have no other
5. from whom to hear them.
6. There will be days
7. when you seek after me
8. and you will not find me.

86
1. Jesus said:
2. The foxes have their dens
3. and the birds have their nest,
4. but the Son of man has no place
5. to lay his head and to rest.

JESUS' DISAPPOINTMENT

65
1. He said:
2. A benevolent man had a vineyard.
3. He gave it to husbandmen
4. so that they would work it
5. and he would receive his produce from their hands.
6. He sent his servant
7. in order that the husbandmen would give him
8. the fruit of the vineyard.
9. They laid hold of his servant,
10. they beat him;
11. a little more and they would have killed him.
12/13. The servant went, he reported to his master.
14. His master said:
15. "Perhaps he did not know them."
16. He sent another servant;
17. the husbandmen beat him also.
18. Then the owner sent his son;
19. he said:
20. "Perhaps they will respect my son."
21. Because those husbandmen realized
22. that he was the heir to the vineyard,
23. they seized him, they killed him.
24. He who has ears let him hear!

JESUS' DISAPPOINTMENT

66

1 *Jesus said:*
2 *Show me the stone*
3 *which the builders have rejected:*
4 *it is the corner-stone.*

There are an appreciable number of sayings in which the disciples or other listeners had come with pre-suppositions or had failed to understand Jesus, and he strives to correct their awareness. There are a few in which he can only challenge them to rise to something better. But in:

A benevolent man had a vineyard   (Logion 65)

and *Show me the stone*   (Logion 66)

he seems almost to have despaired of some of his people—parables of rejection and even killing. Perhaps it might be regarded as the humanity of Jesus to feel disappointment that his Teachings were not being recognized or accepted.

Wise Sayings

25
1. Jesus said:
2. Love your brother even as your own soul,
3. guard him
4. even as the pupil of your eye.

26
1. Jesus said:
2. The mote that is in your brother's eye
3. you see,
4. but the beam that is in your own eye
5. you see not.
6. When you cast the beam out of your eye,
7. then you will see clearly
8. to cast the mote out of your brother's eye

32

1. Jesus said:
2. A city built on a high mountain
3. and made strong
4. cannot fall,
5. nor can it be hidden.

34

1. Jesus said:
2. If a blind man guides the Being of a blind man,
3. both of them fall to the bottom of a pit.

72

1. A man said to him:
2. Tell my brothers
3. to divide my father's possessions with me.
4. He said to him:
5. Oh man, who made me a divider?
6. He turned to his disciples,
7. he said to them:
8. Is it that I am a divider?

95

1 Jesus said:
2 If you have money,
3 do not lend at interest,
4 but give it
5 to him who will not return it.

93

1 Give not what is pure to dogs,
2 lest they cast it on the dung-heap.
3 Throw not pearls to swine
4 lest they pollute them.

The Consummation

1
1. *And he said:*
2. *He who finds the inner meaning of these logia*
3. *will find life independent of death.*

2
Jesus said:
1. *Let him who seeks not cease from seeking*
2. *until he finds;*
3. *and when he finds,*
4. *he will be disturbed,*
5. *and when he is disturbed*
6. *he will marvel*
7. *and he shall reign over the All.*

3

1. Jesus said:
2. If those who guide your Being say to you:
3. "Behold the Kingdom is in the heaven,"
4. then the birds of the sky will precede you;
5. if they say to you: "It is in the sea,"
6. then the fish will precede you.
7. But the Kingdom is in your centre
8. and is about you.
9. When you Know your Selves
10. then you will be Known,
11. and you will be aware that you are
12. the sons of the Living Father.
13. But if you do not Know yourselves
14. then you are in poverty,
15. and you are the poverty.

THE CONSUMMATION

These three opening sayings in this Gospel comprise a summary or quintessence of its teachings. It is apparent that Thomas consolidated them in his mind before he came to dictate the others. Now that you have worked through the individual teachings, you will be enabled to discern the full inner meanings hidden within that opening. In doing this you will pick up and consolidate individual teachings that you have already learnt.

Seek is the word the Gospel starts with, just as seeking is the start of your spiritual journey. Yet the precursor for that is a sincere and ardent urge to seek, to be pursued in the heart by that urge.

Any seeking man or woman who does not cease from such seeking shall find. It is a promise given repeatedly by Jesus that has no conditions, it is unqualified. It involves only yourself and him, there is no intermediary.

However, he warns, you the seeker will be disturbed. This may be likened to no more than a pool of clear water in a mountain steam being troubled. More often it will involve you in leaving behind old luggage from previous teachings. It may mean your becoming detached in your spiritual life from your father and mother, but doing it in his way, as he had to do. It may mean your having the Courage to go out as a monakhos. It most probably means your making the effort to quench the dominance of your ahamkāra. That may come gradually like flour trickling from a broken jar, or it may require the strength and resolution of killing a giant. It may even mean going through a cleansing and refining fire.

But, Jesus encourages you, that this disturbance gives rise to marvelling. He promises you that the wonder of your being emptied of ahamkāra results in a peace, tranquility and repose that goes beyond the power of mere words to express. It is an experience.

Thomas recalls that Jesus can gently lampoon the other guides from the old way. Then he says—speaking with the words his Jewish listeners could grasp—the Kingdom is at your Centre and it is all about you. The access to that Kingdom is to Know—at its deepest meaning—your Real Self. Furthermore, this is a reciprocal knowing, between yourself and the Father. Those two aspects of knowing, a this way and a that way, comprise a duality. Yet as you go higher they merge and they become known as a Oneness.

Jesus gives you the warning that if you have not come to Know —in a very profound sense—your Real Self you will not only live in spiritual poverty, but you will be that poverty itself. Not just impoverished but—the ancient Coptic is quite clear about it— that poverty itself.

Then, as you consider the culmination of the previous saying where Jesus is speaking to his other hearers using the Greek idiom, he refers to that Oneness as the All, which in our modern idiom is the Ultimate or the Ultimate Reality.

When you take these two sayings together, with their two ways of speaking, he or she who finds, is disturbed and marvels, reigns over the All, and becomes King of the Kingdom.

This is the ultimate mystical experience of Oneness whereby, assimilating the words of Jesus you become as him, and he becomes as you. At that Ultimate there can be nothing further, just tranquil joy and happiness exists.

PART III

Reflections

Preface to these Reflections

Having been familiar, for a significant number of years, with the meanings of the sayings in the Gospel of Thomas, and being familiar with the spiritual teachings hidden within it, a number of themes or topics have come to mind. As each one has arisen it has been captured in what may be called a 'Reflection'.

Most often the main substance has come to mind spontaneously. Others have been prompted by reading, or by conversation with friends. Sometimes this has been on waking in the morning. Some have flashed into shape in a moment; others have needed several days of consideration. The general feeling, however, is that the Gospel of Thomas has been working somewhere within, and that its power has manifested in this way.

Some of these Reflections derive from their being a response to ordinary outward topics when seen in the light of the teachings in the Gospel. Others may serve as a means to clarify or emphasize the concepts within it.

You may at first be a little surprised that there is some preponderance of these Reflections being about ahamkāra. They look at it from different view-points. This comes from my own experience. It is the most difficult teaching in this Gospel. It is a concept that is virtually absent from our Western culture. It is so much the opposite to our emphasis on the personality. And it keeps on coming back, in such stealthy ways and in so many different guises. It may well take you several years to grasp its meaning fully, and to deal with its manifestations in your life.

It is in those contexts that these Reflections are shared with you in this book.

Searching and Finding

The Gospel of Thomas is for people who are searching—searching for inner peace, tranquility, timeless certainties, happiness and joyousness in this life, in the here and now. It is for those who at some time in their lives, even if not now, search for answers to mankind's most fundamental questions "From whence did I come? To where will I go?" It may even go some way to give solace to those who search for release from suffering—the greatest scourge of mankind.

The words used in the ancient manuscript are the Coptic ϣⲓⲛⲉ and ϣⲓⲛⲉ-ⲛⲥⲁ which are rendered as 'seek' and 'seek-after'. These occur thirteen times, so this frequent occurrence shows that for Jesus searching was a paramount route to spirituality.

In fact is is more than that, for it provides a motive and direction for that journey. Spiritual awareness comes about not by sitting idle, waiting for something to descend from on high, or for some sudden great revelation to occur spontaneously or be engendered by some charismatic person. As the journey is presented in 'Thomas' you are told a vital constituent is your seeking.

The teaching in 'Thomas' however goes further still. For associated with seeking is finding. Two Coptic words are used ϭⲓⲛⲉ and ⲏⲉ which appear to have the same meaning. These occur no less than twenty-nine times, so from the numerical point of view are the most frequently used in the entire Gospel.

So the message Jesus is trying to give you is that if you are willing to search—in his way—this will be followed by finding.

Let him who seeks not cease from seeking until he finds;
(From logion 2)

There will be days when you seek after me and you will not find me (From logion 38)

Seek and you will find. (From logion 92)

He who seeks shall find, (From logion 94)

Such is the strength in 'Thomas' of this emphasis on finding that is has prompted the use of the word 'shall' in its old English sense of being a command. It is appropriate to feel that when you diligently search in 'Thomas' for the spiritual treasures to be found there you will be commanded to find them.

Treasure Hunt

'You also seek after the treasure' (logion 76.8)

The Gospel of Thomas is a veritable treasure hunt. That is to say, it can be looked on as having all the qualities of a treasure hunt. It announces itself; it tells of its objective; it speaks of the motivation to carry through the hunt; it provides the clues; and itself it gives the treasure.

Right in the opening line it announces that something is hidden 'These are the hidden logia' (#0.1). Something is hidden, but it is not a secret. It is available to all. Here is the clearest possible invitation for you to take part in a treasure hunt.

Almost at once it tells of its objective: 'He who finds the inner meaning of these logia' (#1.2). You are to set off on a voyage of discovery to find something. Without a moment's hesitation the objective of the hunt is proclaimed: 'to find Life independent of death' (#1.3). This is the Life of Jesus the Life-Giver, even though you may each only find it in your own limited way.

But how you may ask, are you to embark on this hunt, this search? Jesus and Thomas do not leave you stranded. The way is made perfectly clear: 'Let him who seeks not cease from seeking' (#2.1). It turns out that seeking was one of the words Jesus very often used. This is what he wishes you to do.

Furthermore, the seeking and the finding are in 'Thomas' intimately connected, for you have not only 'Let him who seeks

TREASURE HUNT

not cease from seeking until he finds' (#2.1&2) but also the promise of 'He who seeks shall find' (#94.2).

You will no doubt recall from your childhood days that in any well-planned treasure hunt the clues were not laid out clearly before you at the start. Part of the action, part of the excitement, was in seeking and searching out the clues themselves, one by one as you went along. So it is in 'Thomas'. The clues themselves are hidden, but only to a limited degree. The finding of them is as much a matter of your approach and attitude of mind as anything, and just keeping your eyes open. Just rest assured that Jesus and Thomas sprinkled their work liberally with clues, make the finding of them a primary objective.

These clues are often quite tiny things. Do not confuse them with the finding of the inner meanings of whole parables, which are on a grander scale. The clues are the means by which you can progress the treasure hunt.

The title of this Reflection shows that there is a treasure to be found. In logion 76 it is likened to the one single pearl for which the wise merchant not only traded in his entire stock but also, by giving up being a merchant, he transformed his whole life. You also are encouraged to find this treasure that not only does not perish but also remains evermore in a certain indestructible place within you.

So what is this treasure, more than a physical, tangible thing that can remain timelessly within, carrying a transforming power? For this you have to take a wider view. Instead of focusing on clues and single sayings, you have to stand back a bit and from a new perspective take in a wider view. When you do that you find that a major theme, represented by the largest group of sayings in the whole Gospel, is the Teaching on Oneness. This, then, is the treasure that our treasure hunt is leading you to, and it is revealed in the Gospel itself.

It becomes the foremost Treasure, which can give you Life independent of death.

A Direct Path Based on Experience

The objective of this 'Reflection' is to provide a Direct Path for you to come to an awareness of the concepts referred to in this book by the names ahamkāra and the Real Self. However this objective can only be achieved with your active co-operation, for it is not to be reached merely by reading and with intellectual understanding, but requires active participation in recalling a series of experiences.

The presentation of this Direct Path has not been found elsewhere in the literature (although there are many indirect or partial references to it) nor does it appear specifically in the words of Jesus in the Gospel of Thomas. Thus he never speaks directly of ahamkāra in the ancient document, although he refers to it indirectly in many ways: as a giant, as a strong man, as a thief and as a band of robbers, as an alien killer, and as a devouring lion. This is one aspect of his practice of speaking symbolically or using analogies.

The first difficulty you have to overcome is that ahamkāra refers to a concept that is absent from our Western culture and therefore no word exists for it in languages such as English or French.

On the other hand, the spiritual culture of India, which we refer to as Hinduism and its derivative Buddhism, is so rich in concepts that its language, Sanskrit, is unequalled in its richness of spiritual words. It has the word ahamkāra for this concept.

Ahamkāra is pronounced with the first, second and fourth a's short as in English apple, and the third ā long as in English car. It is compounded from two words. The first is aham, the first person singular or 'I' in English. The second is kara meaning 'the making of'. Sanskrit has the further feature of combining words so that the compound word has greater meaning than the sum of the constituent words alone. Thus a literal meaning of ahamkāra could be 'the making of I-ness'.

The French Metanoïa scholars have used l'Ego as their name for this concept. Greek 'ego' is exactly equivalent to Sanskrit 'aham' and English 'I'. It has therefore much less meaning than the compound Sanskrit word. So while it is convenient, especially in conversation, to use Ego—when written using a capital E—very great care has to be taken to avoid confusing it with ego as used in psychology or some other contexts. It is found best just to learn the meaning of ahamkāra—one purpose of this 'Reflection'—and to get used to the Sanskrit name.

To start your journey of discovery on this Direct Path look at the diagram on the page opposite. What you find there is a series of words that are familiar to everyone. However, note the heading: Experiences of Life. This is where your crucial participation begins. It is necessary to make the transformation from the words in little boxes into a series of incidents and experiences in your own life. This transformation needs to be done during periods of contemplation, taking one word at a time and recalling from your memory some event or happening that is exactly related to the word. You can take the words in any order or sequence. Perhaps tick each one off when you've recalled its experience. What you are doing is building up a particular collection of your own experiences of your life.

A DIRECT PATH BASED ON EXPERIENCE

The Experiences of Life

- Happiness-or-bliss Joyousness
- Goodness
- Pride
- Hatred Anger
- Envy Greed
- Love Devotion
- Compassion
- Suffering
- Distress Depression
- Courage
- Turmoil Aggression
- Vacillation
- Evil
- Acceptance
- Selfishness Meanness
- Gratitude
- Peacefulness Tranquility
- Competitiveness Assertiveness
- Generosity
- Insights Inspiration
- Steadiness
- Cowardice Fear
- Contentment
- Harshness
- Non-attachment
- Emphasis on the intellect
- Indifference
- Corruption
- Well-being
- Beauty
- Changeableness
- Resolution Certainty

A DIRECT PATH BASED ON EXPERIENCE

On the previous page you will have seen a set of perfectly ordinary English words, each within its little box. If you have been following this Direct Path diligently you will have expanded them into experiences of your life. Each word then becomes a name to point to that experience. In practice it may well take several weeks or even months to do this transformation for any significant number of the words. At least, if it is hurried there will be gaps and potholes in the Direct Path, and your coming to an awareness of ahamkāra and the Real Self will be impaired.

Now you may progress to the next stage of this Path. It is merely the simple task of rearranging the names into pairs, thus:

The Contrasting Pairs

Happiness-or-bliss Joyousness	Well-being	Love Devotion	Compassion
Distress Depression	Suffering	Hatred Anger	Harshness

Generosity	Contentment	Gratitude	Goodness
Selfishness Meanness	Envy Greed	Indifference	Evil

Acceptance	Courage	Steadiness	Peacefulness Tranquility
Competitiveness Assertiveness	Cowardice Fear	Changeableness	Turmoil Aggression

Resolution Certainty	Beauty	Insights Inspiration	Non-attachment
Vacillation	Corruption	Emphasis on the intellect	Pride

154

You will notice that within each pair they are opposites.

In that diagram it is the lower ones of each pair, set in bold heavy type, that are the experiences that belong to the realm of ahamkāra. Ahamkāra consists of those experiences. In your life you have experienced these manifestations of your ahamkāra. Ahamkāra is where the troubles, and most especially the suffering, in your life have lived. Ahamkāra is the domain of all that is dark in your life.

What you are seeing is the experience in your life of the giant, the experience of the strong man, the experience of the robbers, the experience of an alien killer, the experience of the devouring lion. Symbolically, it is the experience of darkness in your life. And it all belongs to ahamkāra, and ahamkāra is where all that belongs.

As you've been going through each and every one of your experiences pointed to by the names in the lower boxes, you've been exercising your ahamkāra, and probably strengthening it. Now is the time to take this matter in hand!

So turn now to the the upper item of each pair, which is set in a light airy style of type. These are experiences of your life that belong to the realm of your Real Self. These labels point to the experiences when you have been witnessing and exercising your Real Self. These symbolically are the experiences of the Light shining in your life. When your Real Self has shone in its splendour.

As you travel this Direct Path towards finding the Light, it becomes obvious that an objective is to diminish the Darkness. But here the exercise of Discrimination, the capability to discern the valuable way from the false, becomes of the greatest importance. Great clarity of thinking is needed.

Most of the manifestations of ahamkāra relate to the physical world, to the body, or to the mind and the senses. It is all too easy to jump to the conclusion that to escape from its clutches the aim is to deny the world, the body and the mind. This thinking leads only to asceticism with all its negativenesses, and there have been many people in the past, and still some today, who have turned to that.

But clearer thinking shows that such denials cannot be reconciled with a recognition of the marvels of being a human being. It is well worth-while to learn something of physiology, the working of our bodies, of the way we assimilate food, of our means to resist the effects of alien substances and infections, and our amazing capacities to heal and to recover health, of both the body and of the mind. Nor, for most people, can it be of benefit to deny the wonder and ecstasy of sexual consummation.

To try to deny the working of the mind runs counter to all the evidence of the great intellectual achievements of mankind. Just consider the great philosophers of the world, the theoreticians upon which our knowledge of the universe is based, the scientists who contribute to our material well-being. No, the mind cannot be denied, it is to be honoured.

It is through the proper use of Discrimination that the distinction can be recognized between a false denial of the realm of ahamkāra and a quenching of the power of ahamkāra. It is the quenching of its power that is important, not the extinguishing of ahamkāra. It is a matter of Discrimination, and it is the way that leads to a full life.

A DIRECT PATH BASED ON EXPERIENCE

During the earlier stages of travelling this Direct Path, as you were recalling from memory those experiences that lie in the lower row of boxes, you were remembering the occasions when you fell prey to the power of your own ahamkāra. It's as simple as that. The value of recognizing it, of learning what is the source of those negative experiences, is that should there be any recurrence you will not be a passive victim but will be forewarned and forearmed.

If the owner of the house is aware
that the thief is coming,
he will stay awake before he comes
and will not allow the thief
to tunnel into his house of his Kingdom
to carry away his goods. . . .
Let there be in your centre a man who is understanding!
(Logion 21)

Happy is the man who knows
where and when the robbers will creep in;
so that he will arise and gather his strength
and prepare for action before they come. (Logion 103)

Jesus teaches you that merely by becoming aware of the source of such troubles you are thereby and automatically given the power to resist and to overcome them, to return to your more natural, more fundamental, condition of living in the positive and finding happiness. This is your Real Self manifesting.

In following this Direct Path, be careful to avoid dwelling on the remembered negative experiences. There are only two values in recalling these to mind. The first is as a means to reveal the working of your own ahamkāra which otherwise remains hidden: one of its very nasty tricks. As to the second, if there may be some future occasion when something similar crops up in your life, let it serve as a pointer, as a prompt, towards the corresponding positive experience. So, if and when such a situation may arise, it might be entirely appropriate to draw in this book an upward arrow as a record of the achievement, using discrimination and your own free-will, of making the transition from the negative world of ahamkāra to the positive world of the Real Self.

Quenching its Power

. . . this which is not yours will kill you.   (From logion 70)

. . . like a man wishing to kill a giant.   (From logion 98)

. . . to enter the house of the strong man   (From logion 35)

. . . if the owner of the house is aware that the thief is coming
(From logion 21)

. . . and abominated is the man whom the lion will eat.
(From logion 7)

With these onerous phrases with their dark symbolic words Jesus seeks to alert you to the power of ahamkāra.

So much in our Western culture works to strengthen it. The emphasis on our tool-making or material attribute, such that we begin to assume and accept that we even have some command over nature. The emphasis in our education on our intellectual attribute, the right side of the brain, to the detriment of the capability of the left side for insights and intuition.

What is more, it is extremely difficult to discern your own ahamkāra. This is one of its most nasty tricks. Because it lies hidden, its power becomes all the greater, becomes more pervasive. So it is a power exercised in secret, always the most powerful.

QUENCHING ITS POWER

Jesus strives to make you aware of your ahamkāra, as do other great spiritual Teachers. By bringing it out into the open, by making it known to you, by giving an example of its absence in order you may assimilate or absorb it, so it is exposed and its power diminished.

But all the time keep your capability for Discernment well honed, as sharp and keen as possible. It is not man's materialistic attribute, the realm of the body, nor his intellectual attribute, the realm of the mind, that is to be diminished. Instead it is their power that is to be brought under control so that your spiritual attribute may come forth and blossom.

. . . .

There is a phrase we are all familiar with 'Forewarned is forearmed'. It must have come from very early tribal days, when a lookout raised the alarm and men dropped whatever they were doing and took up their arms in defence. Yet Jesus used the idea in his sayings and Thomas thought fit to record them in his Gospel.

If the owner of the house is aware
that the thief is coming,
he will stay awake before he comes
and will not allow the thief
to tunnel into his house of his Kingdom
to carry away his goods. . . .
Let there be in your centre a man who is understanding!
(From logion 21)

QUENCHING ITS POWER

Happy is the man who knows
where and when the robbers will creep in;
so that he will arise and gather his strength
and prepare for action before they come. (From logion 103)

What is it that Jesus is referring to? It can only be the giant, the strong man, the thief and band of robbers, the alien killer and the devouring lion—the manifestations of the power of ahamkāra. The value of recognizing it is that should there be any recurrence you will not be a passive victim but will be forewarned and forearmed.

Jesus teaches you that merely by becoming aware of the source of such troubles you are thereby and automatically given the power to resist and to overcome them, to return to your more natural, more fundamental, condition of living in the positive and finding happiness. This is your Real Self becoming manifest.

The Indian Similarity

By the time of Jesus the Indian spiritual tradition was two thousand years old. It had been developed and refined by a series of enlightened men, to reach a very high degree of sophistication. Because the monsoon, with its excessive humidity, tends to impair the longevity of books, the concepts were carried forward in the memories of men. Special groups spent their lives memorizing and recounting the great spiritual records, usually by a form of chanting. Since these records largely take the form of stories, enlightened men who had grasped their inner meanings shared their awareness with followers. Both these practices continue today.

One of the distinctive features of Indian culture makes it possible for individuals of a certain proclivity to spend much of their lives in contemplation. It is an activity—if one can regard it as such—that is considered of the highest worth; such persons are looked on with the greatest respect, admiration and veneration.

A consequence is that particular individuals, it may be only a tiny handful at any one time, develop extraordinary powers. That word is used with both its meanings—these capabilities are out of the ordinary, and they are amazing to normal people. As examples, some can live outside of time, so they may foresee events in the future, and they may live outside the constraints of space, so that distance becomes non-existent for them. We call these extra-sensory perceptions, and such people may be regarded as seers.

As Jesus was growing up to manhood it would be in accord with Indian practice for some of these people with special powers to discern his existence and come to witness him, bringing as offerings something of their spiritual tradition.

One of its features, however, is that it is merely offered. It is never imposed or asserted. It is the very opposite of evangelical Christianity or radical Islam. It is offered, and it is for the recipient to be a seeker in order to accept it. In the Gospel of Thomas Jesus places much emphasis on being a seeker; and what he said may well have been from his own experience of becoming a finder.

Let him who seeks not cease from seeking
until he finds . . . (Logion 2)

He who seeks shall find
and to him who knocks it shall be opened. (Logion 94)

We also have to take into account that just as those carriers of Indian spirituality might travel to come into the presence of Jesus, so in his early manhood he could travel to their homeland to sample it at its source. Certainly at that time there was active traffic between India and the Middle East, not least for purposes of trade. This possibility is supported by the non-Christian records that exist of Jesus travelling to India. Professor Fida Hassnain has diligently studied ancient documents in Kashmir and its neighbour Ladakh, where he found many references to

Jesus living for several years in India, and travelling extensively.* There he would have learnt that spiritual awakening and spiritual awareness is transmitted from highly evolved individuals to those who seek what they have to offer. Such people may be referred to as realized or illuminated or inspiring. A seeker comes to discern a light embodied within them.

In the Gospel of Thomas Jesus frequently speaks of there being Light within a person:

We came from the Light

there, where the Light was, by itself. (Logion 50)

There is Light

at the centre of a man of Light,

and he illuminates the whole world. (Logion 24)

This awareness could not have been some idle speculation. He may have been speaking from his own experience of finding one of these enlightened persons, and his amazement in doing so. It could well have contributed to his saying:

. . . when he finds,

he will be disturbed,

and when he is disturbed

he will marvel. . . . (Logion 2)

---

* He summarizes his findings in his book ISBN 0946551005 and also in his ISBN 9781577332213. See also Holger Kersten's ISBN 1852305509 and Elizabeth Clare Prophet's ISBN 091676687X. You will be surprised and fascinated by this topic and its well-researched supporting facts.

THE INDIAN SIMILARITY

We can find in the Gospel of Thomas several logia that seem to refer to the causes of such a disturbance. In logion 45 (page 86) he decries the rabbis and Temple priests of his youth. In #102 (page 119) and #39 (page 118) he is very critical of the Pharisees, who he may well have visited in Judea. As a seeker he would have visited the Esseenes, a Jewish sect who we know about from the 'Dead Sea Scrolls'.* He may also have sought out the Gnostic groups who were active in his land.

Furthermore, what we find in this Gospel are many logia that are similar to the highest form of Indian spirituality. They can be easily enough identified:

> The teaching on Discrimination;
>
> The replacement of belief and faith by knowing, and especially by Knowing-for-certain;
>
> No emphasis on sin, with its concomitant sense of guilt;
>
> The emphasis on happiness or bliss or joyousness, and even the concept that the Real Self is happiness itself.
>
> In the key-note saying #3 (page 139) which deposes of the idea of the Kingdom being 'out there', whether in the sky or the sea, and replaces it by the emphatic assertion that it may be Known-for-certain to be within.

What, however, would have most amazed him, and most contributed to the creative disturbance of his Jewish birthright,

---

* In his second book ISBN 9781577332213 Professor Fida Hassnain shows there is plenty of evidence that Jesus knew the Esseenes well, and this had important consequences in later events in his life. This is corroborated in the ancient document *The Acts of Thomas*.

THE INDIAN SIMILARITY

would have been to discern in one of the Indian illuminated persons the subjugation and absence of ahamkāra. Returning to his homeland, to share with his own people the insights that had come to him, his sayings recorded in the Gospel of Thomas show this to be a topic that greatly occupied his mind. This awareness of ahamkāra, and by its exclusion that leads to the experience of Oneness, is distinctive of Indian spirituality.

These are concepts entirely alien to the Hebraic background of Jesus' youth, and in the most crucial respects are the very opposite. Just as they are in our Christian background (except for the awareness of certain mystics), so they may have been introduced to him from some other tradition. This suggests that there were qualities in the Indian spiritual tradition and practice that may well have become assimilated into Jesus' awareness of the nature of spiritual Truth.

To put such emphasis in his sayings on the nature of ahamkāra, on its quenching that leads to the experience of Oneness, shows that Jesus may have experienced the presence of one of India's realized enlightened men.

As you become accustomed to the idea of Jesus going to India you may find the glittering possibility that the second, and crucial, saying recorded by Thomas might well be auto-biographical. That could come about if Jesus, in his late twenties, came into the presence of one of those extra-ordinary men in India.

And as you assimilate the last chapter in Part II of this book, The Consummation (it's on page 138), and grasp the meaning of the final phrase of that saying:

. . . he shall reign over the All.

you will realize that Jesus then had the experience of being the King of the Kingdom.

Let him who seeks not cease from seeking
until he finds;
and when he finds,
he will be disturbed,
and when he is disturbed
he will marvel
and he shall reign over the All.

Dwell in the Light

We came from the Light, there, were the Light was,
(From logion 50)

There is Light at the centre of a man of Light (From logion 24)

When he is emptied he will be filled with Light (From logion 61)

. . . the Light will reveal itself (From logion 83)

I am the Light that is above them all (From logion 77)

The primary effect of ahamkāra is to veil the spiritual attribute in you—to veil the Light.

The work in the spiritual is to quench the power of ahamkāra, to control it and to draw back its veil.

Jesus assures you that you came from the Light, that when you empty yourself of ahamkāra that in itself will fill you with Light. He assures you that then you can be filled with Light.

This is your birth-right, this is where you may dwell, this leads to peacefulness and tranquillity, this leads to an awareness of the glory of the Real Self.

Empty Desert ?

The word empty is used three times in the Gospel of Thomas:

. . . that empty they came in to the world

and that empty they seek to go out of the world again

(From logion 28)

. . . and the flour streamed out behind her on the road

. . . she found it empty. (From logion 97)

When he is emptied he will be filled with Light; (Logion 61)

The word in the ancient document we are dealing with here has not only the meaning of emptiness but also is used for an uninhabited desert. It is easy enough to see how those two ideas got combined in the time and place of Jesus.

However, in the language of parables which Jesus used, and his listeners understood, and which we have to rediscover in order that 'Thomas' is truly to speak to us, those ancient words are likely to be used with flexible meanings.

In that language of parables the desert is not empty—it becomes filled.

With what can it be filled? If you were to go into it, devoid of all encumbrances and distractions, it can only be filled by yourself. There can be nothing else.

EMPTY DESERT ?

And what happens when you enter a desert? Such vast spaces create through their immensity an awe, a wonder, and expansion of the Inner Being.

So what is Jesus trying to say to you? There is the removal of something, an emptying, and yet something else is to be found to engender that awe and wonder.

The emptying is the quenching of the power of ahamkāra, and the fulfillment is the finding of your Real Self.

Frequently in 'Thomas' Jesus prompts you in this way. For the fulfillment he uses the words the One and the All. There cannot be anything greater than this, it fills you with the ultimate wonderment.

It is only your ahamkāra that obscures in your daily life the immensity of the indwelling Real Self.

Opening the Door

All the experiences of life that relate to the material, the mental or the emotional belong to the realm of ahamkāra. The material includes all those relating to the body, and all those relating to or derived from objects. Most particularly all suffering in the body or all of what we call the emotion of distress belong to ahamkāra.

Attaching importance to any of the experiences relating to the material, the mental or the emotional is merely the influence of the power of ahamkāra. To regard any of those as significant in your life is merely one of its tricks.

The desert experience of earlier centuries was a means to become detached from the encumbrances of ordinary life. The life of a hermit in his cell in the mountains was a way to be unburdened by material things. The long periods of contemplative retreat by Buddhist masters are means to be purified of material, mental and emotional ties. The ancient practice in the Indian tradition of going out into the forest for the third stage of life—after youth, after being a householder and creating a family—was to find such a freedom. In particular, the experience of Jesus termed 'the temptations in the desert', despite being recorded in the N.T. Gospels in such grossly anthropomorphic terms, was the necessary preparation for his mission.

The greatest discrimination has to be applied here to discern the essential distinctions. Merely to reject the material leads to asceticism, and denies the wonders of our bodies and the glory of the culmination of sexual experience. To reject the mental denies the wonderful human facility to discover the physical laws of science and to establish an understanding of the nature of the universe.

Thus to assume, to imagine or to think that an abnegation of all these experiences is a desirable aim is one of the greatest mistakes that can be made.

Instead, the quenching of the power of ahamkāra has to be used as a means to Open the Door. It is something you can do in the here and now.

This is the doorway to the single large fish chosen by the wise fisherman. To the one sheep treasured more than all the ninety-nine. To the incorruptible treasure which, when found in the field, displaced all the merchant's stock. To the single pearl of great price.

This is the doorway to finding spiritual Truth. To finding the Real Self. To Knowing the Kingdom. To finding the tranquillity of the peace that passeth understanding. To become aware of the One that is beyond all duality. To discern the All beyond which nothing can be. To reign over the All which is the Kingdom itself.

The great Teachers and Sages that have come for the benefit of mankind have found and passed through this door to attain their total control of ahamkāra. That passage released the quality inherent within them, to present it to others. Jesus must be included amongst them. His teachings are made available to us in the Gospel of Thomas; the effects of his charismatic qualities as a Sage on those amongst whom he ministered are recorded in the N.T. Gospels. One who has sat at the feet of a living Teacher and Sage can testify to the illuminating and transforming presence.

The Jewel

Spiritual Truth may be likened to a jewel.

A jewel may have many different names: amethyst, or emerald, or ruby, or topaz, or most of all a diamond—'a girl's best friend'. When it is brought out from its hiding in the earth it seems little more than a pebble, discoloured by earth and grime, perhaps encrusted with hard substances. So it is difficult to discern any value in it.

But ask a craftsman jeweller to work on it, to convert it into a 'brilliant'. He cuts away the encrustations, chips off unwanted parts, and with consummate skill converts it into a distinctive shape.

We are accustomed to seeing a diamond with its large top face. But change your viewpoint to look at it from the side, when you will see that the top surface is surrounded by many facets. While below, the part that is usually hidden in the mounting of the ring or pendant, its shape is an inverted pyramid.

When you use some of your knowledge of physics, you will learn that light passes into the jewel through that large top face, is reflected from the surfaces of the inverted pyramid, and emerges again from the facets around the periphery. Because of the refracting qualities of a jewel, that light is transformed into the colours of the spectrum. Thus that light manifests as the myriad, varied, magical, flashes of coloured light that emanate from the facets that surround the jewel.

THE JEWEL

Let us now consider an analogy, one of the classic means to reach to the spiritual truth.

Spirituality goes under many different names: the Truth, or the Ultimate, or Ultimate Reality, or Reality, or Oneness. Jesus in the Gospel of Thomas calls it the Kingdom, or the kingdom of heaven, or the Father, or the Mother, or the All or the One. In the language of the great Indian spiritual tradition, Sanskrit, it is called the Atman or Sat-Chit-Ananda.

In its form as the spiritual attribute in mankind—the third, the greatest, the highest of these distinctive attributes—it lies hidden within you, present, pre-existent, latent, waiting to be found. As it struggles towards your awareness it comes out encrusted by all the dross and distractions of ahamkāra, these hardened by your being accustomed and dependent on them for many years.

But lay it before a Great Soul. He will help you to change your viewpoint, look at it from a different perspective. He will encourage and help you to become aware of the wily, stealing, ways of ahamkāra, give you the strength and the courage to chip away at its deceptions, its false attractions, its beastly veiling qualities, so that the Light may enter it.

That Light will not only warm you inwardly. It is transformed in most wonderful ways. It comes out through the facets of your Being as the experiences of happiness and joyousness, of love and compassion, of peace and tranquillity, of repose, of generosity, of gratitude, of certainty and Knowing, of stability and assurance and strength, of courage and fearlessness, of awareness of beauty.

With the help of a Great Soul, your Best Friend, the Spiritual becomes your Experience itself.

The Inherent Light Within

The Light (always spelled with a capital letter in this context) is the word Jesus used to refer to the emanation, the manifestation, of the spiritual attribute in mankind. It is not the attribute itself, for which he uses Father, Kingdom, the One, the All, but a radiation that comes from the attribute.

In two of the sayings in which Jesus was addressing his disciples we have:

We came from the Light
there, where the Light was,
by itself. (From logion 50)

There is Light
at the centre of a man of Light, (From logion 24)

So this light is initially associated with, is a component of, mankind. Furthermore, it was self-existent, it came into being as part of the distinctive evolution of mankind, it is an essential component of man's nature.

Specially when you are cluttered up and burdened with the affairs of the material world and your outward concerns, it is difficult to recognize this. It is during times of stillness and contemplation that you can become aware that Great Souls such as Jesus not only embodied this quality but also sought to share an awareness of it with others. It is through the medium of the radiation of the Light that this awareness is communicated to you, the warmth of its radiance to kindle a fire within.

In that glow of that presence you can come to the true Life in the here and now, finding peace, repose and the happiness that is your real nature.

A Sparkling Analogy

In the great Indian spiritual tradition, the way awareness of spiritual Truth is passed from teacher to seeker is by means of stories and by analogies. One such analogy is that spiritual Truth can be likened to a splendid jewel. Just like a great jewel, that Truth is also a treasure. Such a jewel when it is cut by a skilled craftsman has a multitude of facets. Each one of these facets represents a component of spiritual Truth.

We have to accept that Jesus was familiar with this jewel and all its facets. We also have the amazing situation that, instead of hugging this jewel to himself, he was motivated to share its treasures with those he moved amongst.

One way in which he did this sharing was by means of his speaking. We can visualize that some, at least, of his sayings stemmed from and embodied one or more of the facets of his jewel. It is those glimpses or reflections of those facets that form the kernel or heart of each of his sayings. As you work, and sometimes struggle, with the outward forms of his sayings you tend to attach importance to that. But you are told in logion #1 that it is the 'hidden' meaning or the kernel that is really the important thing to find:

He who finds the inner meaning of these logia
will find Life independent of death.

A SPARKLING ANALOGY

Once you see that the quest is to find the kernel in each saying, it will be realized that the outer form of the saying takes on the nature of a shell or husk.*

In both the Indian practice and also in 'Thomas' the intended meaning of the analogy or parable is not spelled out. This is because in our analogy of the cut jewel with many facets each element of spiritual Truth cannot be captured in mere words, all that the words can do is to point towards what the facet represents.

It was the skill of Jesus to be able to do this. And we see that this skill went further because he surrounded each kernel with the outer husk, giving what we call his parables. This was the way Jesus shared in speech—with those who could hear him—his awareness of spiritual Truth. We may reflect with wonder at his ability to create words that say two things at once, one simple and the other profound.

It is our good fortune that Thomas understood both the inner and the outer parts of many of these sayings and had the motivation to record them. That good fortune has spanned across nearly two millennia, for the sayings to become available to us.

To benefit from Jesus' gracious sharing of his spiritual awareness, it is your task to seek to find the kernel hidden within its husk of each saying. But in doing so you have to recognize that you will not be finding something pinned down in words. Rather, with due diligence the facet that Jesus was sharing becomes an experience within. These are experiences that will not be

---

* It follows from this that the practice of making comparisons and contrasts between the sayings in 'Thomas' and those in the N.T. Gospels, which is so abundantly prevalent in the contributions on the internet, is only dealing with the outward forms, the husks, of Jesus' sayings.

forgotten. Gradually, as you find, facet by facet, these glimpses, you can accumulate them within yourself and approach the sparkling treasure that Jesus sought to share with each of us.

The dynamic spiritual power that radiates from a great Soul is the Light. In written form it has to be spelled with a capital letter; it is represented in our sixth-century icon of Jesus as a halo. When you prepare yourself to permit this to enter you it circulates within as a glowing, warming power. That enriches and nourishes. As it grows in intensity you too can share it with others—logion 24:

There is Light

at the centre of a man of Light,

and he illumines the whole world.

A sparkling diamond is often chosen as an engagement ring. That engagement is a prelude, an announcement, a promise of a forthcoming marriage. In the website can be found this inspired commentary by the French Métanoïa scholars (logion 24):

"The marriage place is where the illusion of duality ceases; but it ceases not by the fusion of two entities, since the One is alone, it ceases through the intuitive knowledge that nothing exists except Him, and that I am no other than Him."

Beyond Any Words

In your spiritual journey guided by 'Thomas' you will find Jesus using a whole group of words of closely related meaning. They include Lord, Kingdom, Father and Mother too, the One, the All. To those we might add our modern words Ultimate Reality, the Ultimate or even just Reality. These are all referring to a Something at the highest spiritual level. It is at the highest level attainable by mankind.

These are not synonyms in the strict sense. On the one hand it is possible that Jesus might have used them interchangeably, to replace one by another while still expressing his thoughts. On the other hand it is clear that his choice of word was dependent on the meaning that his hearers would give to it. Thus father and mother would be appropriate for hearers for whom the family was the most important thing they knew. Kingdom would convey the idea of the most splendid aspect of a tribe or petty kingdom. Lord would make sense to a person coming from the great Jewish tradition. The One, the All, were appropriate for his Hellenistic hearers coming from the sophisticated and philosophical culture of the Greeks. It might even help you, whenever you come across one of these words in his sayings, to convert it into 'the Absolute'.

The first crucial point to grasp is that these are not names, they are not labels to try to attach to that Something. In fact, it is impossible to use a word or attach a label because the Something includes all words within itself. Words that are only part of something cannot describe or define the whole.

The second crucial concept to grasp is that all these words are merely pointers. They do not relate to the Something itself, but point towards something that is beyond and above each of them. The third crucial idea is that it is important and even necessary to leave the pointers behind on your spiritual journey, to free yourself from any attachment to them in order to go further.

The spiritual journey you are embarked on is to become aware inwardly of what that something is, to a lesser or greater extent. It thus becomes an experience, and is most likely to be found during times of contemplation, especially if that is a focused contemplation. It is just possible you might be able to find someone who embodies or displays that quality to a high degree, when it will automatically resonate with what is innate in you, waiting to be awakened. Then it becomes not merely an experience of something, but is Experience itself. The ultimate Experience—to a lesser or greater degree—for you as a member of mankind.

Removing the Mountain

*If two make peace with each other in this single house,
they will say to the mountain "Move away"
and it shall move.* (Logion 48)

Another saying,* logion 106, is very similar, even using some of the same phrases, and certainly carrying the same meaning.

Jesus uses the word 'house' in the Gospel of Thomas with an entirety symbolic meaning. It does not mean your home or dwelling. It means the totality of your Being, all of the three attributes of mankind, both your Real Self and your ahamkāra. He even calls that your "single house", all that collected together. He also uses the word 'mountain' in a similar symbolic way. So you have to ask yourself what he means by that.

It can only refer to the greatest obstacle or impediment to your life of happiness, the greatest burden you may have to bear. That is suffering.

Suffering can arise in the body, as a signal that all is not well and functioning properly, when we call it pain. Or it may occur in the

---

* Thomas, as the 'twin' of Jesus, certainly did understand the meaning and the significance of Jesus' sayings. The fact that he included two so similar, and quite far apart in his original text, indicates that Jesus spoke several times on this topic.

mind and the senses when we call it distress or anguish. Especially when these are beyond the help of medicine they can be acute.

Yet the body, and also the mind and the senses, both belong to the realm of ahamkāra. They even belong exclusively to that realm. So also does suffering. The intensity of suffering merely shows the power of ahamkāra

It has been said that spirituality is in the world, but is not of the world. In just the same way it may be said that the Real Self is in the body and mind but is not of the body and mind. In that way suffering is put in its place.

In times of pain or distress, it may be of help to ponder on those ideas.

So what Jesus is here urging upon you in these two sayings is to make peace between your ahamkāra and your Real Self. This can only be done by quenching the power of ahamkāra. To do that requires Courage, which itself belongs to the realm of the Real Self, which is happiness itself.

You can get at this another way. Symbolically, the Real Self can be represented by light, and ahamkāra by darkness. Light can overcome darkness, but darkness cannot overcome light.*

---

* The second of the two sayings, logion 106, uses the obscure phrase "Son of man". It can only mean one in whom light has overcome darkness, the Real Self has overcome the power of ahamkāra.

The Big Question—Or Is It ?

An enlightened author Francis Clark brings to our notice[23] Emperor Hadrian's dying thoughts. Hadrian knew of the religious and philosophical traditions of his vast empire—those of Rome and Greece, Zoroastrians, Egyptian, something of Indian, the Germanic tribes, the Celts, Jews and Christians, the mystery religions of Mythras, Isis, Dionysius and Eleusinian. In his last days he composed an 'Address to the Soul':

Little soul, trembling soul, fond little soul,

Guest and partner of my body,

To what realms must you now go forth

Little soul, pale, palsied, stripped bare?

There you can no more be merry, as here you love to be.

Clark continues in the same vein, writing with great sensitivity and compassion:

"There is something universal, timeless and creedless in Hadrian's poignant little stanza. Lament for mortality is an ever-sounding ground-bass of human experience. Sooner or later all men and women come face to face with the fact of death—whether by presence at the death of others, or at least in the certain prospect of their own death. The loss of a loved one, the impression made by sudden tragedy, the advance of age and infirmity—these raise insistently questions which are not merely speculative but urgently practical and personal. Is my existence coming to a meaningless dead-end? Am I to go out like a snuffed candle? What is to become of this finely-spun web of consciousness, my joys and hopes, my knowledge and resolves, my very self? Although in my mind I span the universe, and I seek truth and values which transcend the world of matter, am I after all nothing but a temporary aggregation of matter, which will return to dust like a leaf when it falls from a tree? Is all communion with other selves to be dissipated like smoke? What of those whom I see die, those I have loved and lost? What happens in that mysterious moment when this life ceases? Who can give a certain answer to these unanswerable questions?"

These are not unanswerable questions, for you have been given the answers by a Great Soul who can now be heard as your Teacher:

Tell us in what way our end will be? . . .

In the Place where the beginning is,

there will be the end.

Happy is he who will stand boldly at the beginning,

he shall know the end, . . .   (From logion 18)

In 'Thomas' the answer given by Jesus to the Ultimate Question is that at your Centre you come from the Light, and you will return and merge with the Light.

A Creative Mantra

Logion 42 has the unique quality of such brevity that it precludes all dross, it is purified like gold in an alchemist's crucible. In the ancient document it comprises only two words, literally the Coptic for 'to become' and the rarely used Greek word 'to pass by' or 'to pass away'. Each, as usual, is accompanied by prefixes and suffixes.

It is possible that the subtle flexibility of Jesus' thought may have intentionally given it two meanings. This flexibility derived from a quality of the Aramaic language, Jesus' mother tongue. Many Aramaic words carry a cluster of meanings; these are not exactly synonyms but are all related, usually at a subtle level.

This saying may well have been given to Jesus' closest disciples as a form of mantra, a phrase given by a teacher to a follower as a window to the spiritual, that can be repeated again and again until it takes root within. At one spiritual level this mantra might have been intended to carry the meaning:

Become yourselves, while passing by.

There are even other sayings by Jesus elsewhere in which you are urged to pass by, to lay aside, worldly and material considerations.

At another spiritual level, which you are more likely to reach further along your spiritual path, it can carry a deeper meaning:

Become your Real Self, as ahamkāra passes away.

A CREATIVE MANTRA

The profound significance of this is that *nothing else* is needed.

Whatever may have been the purpose and the meaning that Jesus intended by this saying, you will be able to find that by the practice of keeping it in your mind and saying it to yourself frequently, whenever a moment arises when you are not encumbered with the worldly affairs of living, it will work as a mantra and have a transforming effect on your life. Thereby you will be reaching the Life and its foremost blessing of happiness-or-bliss and joyousness, for that is what lies at your Centre.

Bibliography and Notes

1) The following source-books were of especial value for making the basic translation of the ancient Coptic and Greek manuscript of the Gospel of Thomas that is given in the calligraphed pages of this book. They are all rare. Only a few are in print, and several of them are not even likely to be found in libraries.

'The Gospel According to Thomas' by A Guillaumont, H-Ch Puech, G Quispel, W Till and Yassah 'Abd Al Mas-ih. Published 1959 and 1976 by E Brill, Leyden, Holland. Professor Quispel first identified the Gospel of Thomas and brought photographs of the manuscript to the West. These scholars were the first to make good the small defects, and translate it into a European language. They identified the individual sayings, and gave the numbers to them.

'L'Évangile Selon Thomas' by Phillipe de Suarez. Published 1975 by Association Métanoïa, 26200, Montélimar, France. This has the unique value of providing a concordance, in French, Coptic and Greek, of all the words used in the Gospel of Thomas; it also gives cross-references to entries in the great dictionaries. I have made my own concordance, in card-index form, in English, Coptic and Greek, of the words used in my translation.

'Évangile Selon Thomas' by É Gillabert, P Bourgeois and Y Haas. Published 1979 by Association Métanoïa. Although with the same title and publishers as the foregoing, and using the same translation of the Gospel into French, this is entirely different. It is noteworthy in giving many of the inner meanings of the sayings, which are written in very erudite French. The 1979 version has the unique and very special value of giving a word-by-word interlinear translation from the Coptic and Greek

into French. Inexplicably the 1994 reprint omits that. The Association Métanoïa scholars identified the short Semitic phrases, and gave them the phrase-numbers. They also established a comprehensive set of cross-references to sayings in the Bible. These are given in my book *'Thirty Essays on the Gospel of Thomas'*.

'The Nag Hammadi Library in English' edited by J M Robinson, translations of the Coptic texts by T O Lambdin. Published 1977 by E J Brill. This is the definitive treatment of all the other books found at Nag Hammâdi.

'A Coptic Dictionary' by W E Crum. Published 1962 by Oxford University Press. Coptic, English and Greek. A majestic life-time's work by an Oxford don. I have made a sub-set of this with only the Coptic words used in the Gospel of Thomas.

'An Introductory Coptic Grammar (Sahidic Dialect)' by J M Plumley. Published 1948 by Home & van Thal, London. Rather than being set in type, the whole of this is photo-reproduced from a hand-written manuscript.

'An Elementary Coptic Grammar of the Sahidic Dialect' by C C Walters. Published 1983 by Blackwell, Oxford, England. This is photo-reproduced from a typescript.

'A Greek-English Lexicon of the New Testament and Other Early Christian Literature' translated and adapted by W F Arndt and F W Gingrich from the German work by Walter Bauer. Published 1957 by University of Chicago Press, USA. I have made a sub-set of only the Greek words used in the Gospel of Thomas.

The ancient manuscript of the Gospel of Thomas is made available photographically in *'The Facsimile Edition of the Nag Hammâdi Codices'*, Brill, 1974 to 1978. With an *'Introduction'* volume. Complemented by a series of volumes on each of the Codices, published up to 1989. The Gospel of Thomas is in Codex II, folios 32 – 51; on page 4 is another photograph showing the whole ancient volume opened at folios 50 and 51.

BIBLIOGRAPHY AND NOTES

(Unfortunately, the photographs of the last page of the Gospel of Thomas are poor.)

2) From Prelim page i

All later icons of Jesus, even modern ones, are clearly based on this, as befitting the tradition of iconography. But there is a major difference: this does not have a crucifix superimposed on the halo. That may derive from the practice of the related early Syrian Church giving Jesus the epithet of the Life-Giver, rather than the Saviour.

3) From Introduction page 3

See the chapter 'The Rôle of Thomas' in my companion book *'Introduction to the Gospel of Thomas'*.

4) From Practical Matters page 10

You will also find it very revealing to write out in long-hand any saying that specially interests or puzzles you.

5) From Practical Matters page 11

This theme is expanded upon in the chapter 'The Words of a Master' in my *Introduction to the Gospel of Thomas*

6) From Practical Matters page 12

See the chapter 'The Church that treasured the Gospel of Thomas' in my *'Thirty Essays on the Gospel of Thomas*

7) From Spirituality, the Ultimate Attribute page 13

Part-way along this progression is all the aspects of home-making, together with everything we make that contribute to our bodily and material well-being.

8) From Spirituality, the Ultimate Attribute page 13

Our spiritual attribute seeks to objectify itself as gods and spirits. These have the immense benefit of being objects for adoration, devotion, respect —all manifestations of the attribute.

BIBLIOGRAPHY AND NOTES

9) From Spirituality, the Ultimate Attribute page 15

There's much more on this theme in the chapter 'The Rôle of Thomas' in my *'Thirty Essays'* book.

10) From Spirituality, the Ultimate Attribute page 15

This is the theme of the chapter 'The Church that treasured . . .' in my *'Thirty Essays'* book. At the end of the chapter there is a valuable bibliography.

11) From Direct Way Forward page 17

All this is reflected in 'Joseph's Recollections' in my *'Thirty Essays'* book. It corresponds to my own experience.

12) From The Summary page 24

It is a great mistake to think of these sayings as being secret, or esoteric, or only for a chosen few, already initiates of some mystery. Sometimes they are referred to as secret sayings, a simple mistranslation of the Coptic.

13) From The Summary page 24

There are other ancient documents purporting to be revealed from a resurrected Christ. This is not one of those.

14) From The Summary page 25

An important point about the initial translation of Jesus' sayings by Thomas is considered in the chapter 'The Rôle of Thomas' in my *'Thirty Essays'* book.

15) From The Summary page 25

The complete collections of sayings, in the order they occur in the ancient Gospel, comprises the main content of my book *'The Gospel of Thomas'*.

BIBLIOGRAPHY AND NOTES

16) From Seeing the Master page 37

The earliest icon of Jesus, which is used for the cover of this book, is made available on the internet at www.gospelofthomas.info/icon. Although that computer-enhanced image is copyrighted, permission is given for you to print it out for your personal use.

17) From To Know and Metanoia page 47

Strictly, the heading of the chapter should use the verb form of the Greek word, *metanoiō*, and it is this that is used in the ancient document. However the noun form, *metanoïa*, which might be translated as 'a transformation of your Knowing', is how the concept is usually referred to, and thus will be more easily recognized here.

18) From Quenching Ahamkāra page 65

Strictly, when using our letters this should be spelled ahankāra, but it is found easier to use ahamkāra. It is a Sanskrit double-word, aham meaning 'I' and kara meaning 'the making of'. So a literal translation might be 'the making of I-ness'.

19) From Quenching Ahamkāra page 70

The Coptic here is difficult to translate exactly. That need not trouble you, the effect or consequence is what is important.

20) From Quenching Ahamkāra page 70

This is expanded upon in the 'Reflection' titled 'Empty Desert ?'

21) From Quenching Ahamkāra page 70

Irina Tweedie in *'The Chasm of Fire'* (Element Books, 1988) tells vividly of her experience of going through the fire as her ahamkāra was quenched by a contemporary spiritual Teacher. Three times Jesus heaped fire upon Peter (Matthew 16:23, Luke 22:34, logion 114 here), yet later he 'wept bitterly' (Luke 2:62) and then came through it (John ch 21). Paul never met Jesus in person to have his abundant ahamkāra burnt up.

BIBLIOGRAPHY AND NOTES

22) From Happiness page 110

The word translated here as 'happy' comes from the Greek word *makarios* in the ancient manuscript. We have no record of the Amharic words Jesus used when speaking to his Jewish hearers. However it is very probable that he used the corresponding word *tubwayhun* (when written with our letters).

Tubwayhun has a great cluster of meanings. In our language these include happiness, bliss, blessed, healthy, aligned with the cosmos, ripe and delighted; where delighted suggests great happiness, prosperity and abundant goodness.

This is just one example of the extreme flexibility of the Amharic language. Anyone's language greatly influences his way of thinking. It's therefore of little wonder that in 'Thomas' we find Jesus using a variety of words to express each of his spiritual concepts.

It also illustrates our extreme good fortune that it was Thomas, who must have been bi-lingual to earn his two nicknames of 'twin', who first translated Jesus' sayings given in Amharic into the Greek in which his Gospel was initially recorded.

23) From The Big Question - Or Is It? page 184

From the Open University course *'Man's Religious Quest'*. Course 208, unit 32, page 10, 1978.

24) You will find it interesting to visit the website on the internet at www.gospelofthomas.info, and also to learn about the other books of our 'Thomas Collection' in another website at www.gospelofthomas.net. The unmanageable quantity of information on the internet about the Gospel of Thomas can be made more digestible by taking note only of those contributions that focus on the meanings of the sayings rather than on the form and nature of the sayings themselves, and all the theories about them.

Index to the Sayings

This Index gives the page references of all the sayings in the order they appear in the original 'Thomas' Gospel.

0	*These are the hidden logia*	page 22
1	*He who finds the inner meaning of these logia*	22 & 138
2	*Let him who seeks not cease from seeking*	22 & 138
3	*If those who guide your Being say to you*	23 & 42 & 139
4	*The man old in days will not hesitate*	73
5	*Know Him who is before your face*	31 & 43
6	*His disciples questioned, they said to him:*	89
7	*Happy is the lion which the man will eat*	64 & 107
8	*The Man is like a wise fisherman*	26 & 87
9	*Behold, the sower went out.*	93
10	*I have cast fire upon the world,*	55 & 63
11	*This heaven will pass away*	76
12	*We realize you will go away from us;*	91
13	*Make a comparison to me*	35
14	*If you fast you will beget a sin to yourselves*	28
15	*When you behold Him who was not begotten of woman*	32
16	*Perhaps men think I have come to cast tranquility upon the earth*	101
17	*I will give you what no eye has seen*	31
18	*Tell us in what way our end will be*	49 & 107
19	*Happy is he who already was before he is*	50 & 108
20	*Tell us, what is the Kingdom of the heavens like?*	88
21	*Mary said to Jesus: whom do your disciples resemble?*	60
22	*Jesus saw children who were being suckled.*	75 & 111 & 125
23	*I will choose you, one out of a thousand*	78

INDEX TO THE SAYINGS

24	*Show us the Place where you are*	52
25	*Love your brother even as your own soul,*	135
26	*The mote that is in your brother's eye*	135
27	*If you transcend not the world of objects,*	128
28	*I stood boldly in the midst of the world,*	46 & 63
29	*If the flesh has come into being because of the spirit,*	127
30	*The place where there are three gods*	78
31	*No prophet is accepted in his own village;*	130
32	*A city built on a high mountain*	136
33	*What you will hear in one ear*	52
34	*If a blind man guides the Being of a blind man*	117 & 136
35	*It is not possible to enter the house of the strong man*	59
36	*Have no care, from morning to evening*	28
37	*On which day will you be manifest to us*	57
38	*Many times you have longed to hear these logia*	132
39	*The Pharisees and the scribes took the keys of knowledge*	118
40	*A vine was planted without the Father*	85
41	*He who has in his hand,*	85
42	*Become your Real Self, as ahamkāra passes away.*	64
43	*Who are you that you should say these things to us?*	119
44	*He who blasphemes against the Father,*	86
45	*Grapes are not harvested from thorn trees*	86
46	*From Adam until John the Baptist*	43 & 117
47	*It is impossible for a man to mount two horses,*	121
48	*If two make peace with each other*	74
49	*Happy are the monakhos and the chosen*	101 & 108
50	*If they say to you: "Where are you from?"*	53 & 112
51	*On which day will the repose of the dead come about?*	99
52	*Twenty-four prophets spoke in Israel*	118
53	*Is circumcision beneficial or not?*	120
54	*Happy are the poor,*	89 & 106
55	*He who does not turn away from his father and his mother*	102

INDEX TO THE SAYINGS

56	*He who has known the world*	128
57	*The Kingdom of the Father is like a man*	92
58	*Happy is the man who has toiled to lose ahamkāra*	56
59	*Look upon Him who is living*	32
60	*They saw a Samaritan carrying a lamb,*	98
61	*Two will rest there upon a couch:*	62
62	*I tell my mysteries to those who are worthy of my mysteries*	80
63	*There was a rich man who had much wealth.*	97
64	*A man had guests and when he had prepared the dinner*	93
65	*A benevolent man had a vineyard.*	133
66	*Show me the stone which the builders have rejected*	134
67	*He who understands the All,*	80
68	*Happy are you when you are disliked*	49 & 105
69	*Happy are they who have been pursued in their heart*	44 & 105
70	*When you bring forth that in yourselves,*	57
71	*I will overturn this house*	56
72	*Tell my brothers to divide my father's possessions with me.*	79 & 136
73	*The harvest is indeed great,*	130
74	*Lord, there are many standing around the well*	130
75	*There are many standing at the door.*	102
76	*The Kingdom of the Father is like a man, a merchant,*	27 & 79
77	*I am the Light that is above them all.*	34 & 81
78	*Why did you come forth to the country?*	44 & 91
79	*A woman from the multitude said to him:*	33
80	*He who has known the world*	128
81	*He who has become rich,*	92
82	*He who is near to me is near to the fire,*	33
83	*The images are manifest to man*	113
84	*In the days when you see your resemblance*	113
85	*Adam came into being from a great power*	95
86	*The foxes have their dens*	132
87	*Wretched is the body that depends on a body.*	77

INDEX TO THE SAYINGS

88	*The angels with the prophets will come to you*	77
89	*Why do you wash the outside of the cup?*	29 & 78
90	*Come to me, for easy is my yoke*	99 & 109
91	*Tell us who you are so that we may believe in you.*	45 & 131
92	*Seek and you shall find.*	131
93	*Give not what is pure to dogs,*	137
94	*He who seeks shall find,*	89
95	*If you have money, do not lend at interest,*	137
96	*The Kingdom of the Father is like a woman, who took a little leaven,*	88
97	*The Kingdom of the Father is like a woman who was carrying a jar full of flour*	58
98	*The Kingdom of the Father is like a man wishing to kill a giant*	58
99	*Your brothers and your mother are standing outside.*	90
100	*They showed Jesus a gold coin*	41
101	*He who does not turn away from his father and mother*	40 & 126
102	*Woe to them, the Pharisees!*	119
103	*Happy is the man who knows*	59 & 106
104	*Come and let us pray today and let us fast!*	40
105	*He who Knows the Father and the Mother*	45 & 126
106	*When you make the two One,*	74
107	*The Kingdom is like a shepherd*	26
108	*He who drinks from my mouth*	34
109	*The Kingdom is like a man who owned in his field a hidden treasure,*	54
110	*He who has found the world*	95
111	*The heavens and the earth will roll back before you,*	55
112	*Woe to the flesh that depends upon the soul!*	77
113	*On which day will the Kingdom come?*	100
114	*Simon Peter said to them: Let Mary go out from amongst us,*	124

Annex – The 'Thomas' Collection

For spiritual seekers and those dissatisfied with the teachings of the established Church, the Gospel of Thomas Collection is a series of spiritual writings that provide unique explanations and insights into Jesus' teachings in that Gospel.

This Collection unveils new depths of spiritual meaning and understanding of these powerful sayings of Jesus.

An important part of the Collection is the valuable website at www.gospelofthomas.info. You will find much more information in that.

There is also the website of the inspiring Commentaries translated from the French Métanoïa scholars, and also the 'Thomas' Web-Zine in www.gospelofthomas.net,

The Gospel of Thomas

This book lies at the heart of the Gospel of Thomas Collection. Its translations are used in all the other books.

It comprises a rigorous translation from the Coptic and Greek of the ancient manuscript. It is independent and uninfluenced by any extraneous concepts.

As the meanings of the sayings have become better understood over the years, minor changes have been made to certain details. These have resulted in successive editions of the published book, this being the fourth. It has thus had a long life.

It is this dynamic quality in the work that underlies its being regarded as a classic translation of the Gospel.

The text of the Gospel is preceded by an Introduction, and is followed by Paraphrases or more liberal translations to help you with some sayings that might be difficult. A full set of Notes follow to give much detailed information on the meaning of specific Coptic words and phrases

Available from any bookstore, quoting ISBN 978-1-84293-135-0 in UK, or ISBN 978-1-84293-184-9 in USA. Available on the internet from Amazon

Introducing the Gospel of Thomas

This short book is intended for you if you are coming to the Gospel of Thomas for the first time. It serves to give you much background information about the Gospel and its origins. Without that, you would be prey to all sorts of speculative and unhelpful ideas that are bandied about.

It is an introductory complement to the present book. The two keep each other company. It gives you all the factual information you need to know about the Gospel of Thomas, but which would be out of place in this book.

It describes the ancient document itself, and the murderous adventures associated with its discovery. It tells of the rôle of Thomas, and considers the ancient Church that grew up based on the Gospel. It highlights the distinctive nature of the words of a Master, an important aspect of the authenticity of the Gospel, and Jesus' use of synonyms and parables. And it gives due prominence to seeking, to knowing, to repose and to happiness.

Available from any bookstore, quoting ISBN 978-07552-1166-1. Available on the internet from Amazon, and available as an e-book from the publisher AuthorsOnline.

Thirty Essays on the Gospel of Thomas

This book covers much the same ground as *Introducing the Gospel of Thomas* while discussing more fully certain topics which other writers are undecided about. In particular, it is the only book in this Collection to include comparisons with corresponding sayings in the New Testament gospels. This is based on the work of the Jesuit scholar Phillipe de Suarez of the French Association Métanoïa.

Two of the Essays expand upon the topics of ahamkāra and the Real Self, which experience shows to be the most difficult for anyone brought up and living in our Western culture.

It also contains a soliloquy by Joseph, the father of Jesus, as he thinks back on his eventful life. While imaginary, it is based on what is revealed by the gospels of Thomas and in the New Testament, together with other reliable sources.

It is available in any bookshop in UK or USA quoting ISBN 978-1-904808-12-1, or from Amazon on the internet.

Jesus untouched by the Church

The author discovered, by means of an experiment, that when the sayings in the Gospel of Thomas are grouped together with like-for-like meanings, a coherent set of spiritual teachings of Jesus are revealed.

This approach has proved to be a unique method of revealing the content of the Gospel. It has also served to reveal practical and spiritual teachings of Jesus that were not apparent before.

This book makes it possible to come very near those who sat in the presence of Jesus, who listened intently to his conversations with his disciples. Jesus becomes a spiritual Teacher in a way that was not apparent before.

It has proved to be of great value to many persons seeking to enrich their spiritual lives with this Gospel. It had a life of eleven years, running out of print at the end of 2009.

It is superseded by the present book, which uses the same version of all the sayings from the ancient document. These are translated to be as helpful as possible for you, and are presented in the same beautiful hand-drawn calligraphy.